People to Know

Billy Graham

World-Famous Evangelist

Sara McIntosh Wooten

Enslow Publishers, Inc.

40 Industrial Road   PO Box 38
Box 398   Aldershot
Berkeley Heights, NJ 07922   Hants GU12 6BP
USA   UK
http://www.enslow.com

Library of Congress Cataloging-in-Publication Data

Wooten, Sara McIntosh.
    Billy Graham : world-famous evangelist / Sara McIntosh Wooten.
       p. cm. — (People to know)
    Includes bibliographical references and index.
    ISBN 0-7660-1533-5
    1. Graham, Billy, 1918- . —Juvenile literature. 2. Evangelists—United
States—Biography—Juvenile literature. [1. Graham, Billy, 1918- . 2. Evangelists.]
I. Title. II. Series.
  BV3785.G69 W66 2000
  269'.2'092—dc21
                         00-009330

Printed in the United States of America

10 9 8 7 6 5 4 3 2 1

To Our Readers:
We have done our best to make sure all Internet addresses in this book were active and appropriate when we went to press. However, the author and the publisher have no control over and assume no liability for the material available on those Internet sites or on other Web sites they may link to. Any comments or suggestions can be sent by e-mail to comments@enslow.com or to the address on the back cover.

Illustration Credits: Archives of the Billy Graham Center, Wheaton, Il., p. 74; Billy Graham Evangelistic Association, pp. 4, 9, 16, 26, 32, 40, 54, 57, 59, 61, 65, 69, 77, 79, 84, 91, 95, 96; Everett/CSU Archives, p. 87; Photofest, p. 52.

Cover Illustration: Billy Graham Evangelistic Association.

Contents

Billy Graham

"Puff Graham"

A tired Billy Graham arrived at the revival tent in Los Angeles to prepare for one of the last nights of his crusade there. A crusade is a religious rally where people gather to hear a dynamic Christian preacher. It was 1949, and for a month Graham had preached night after night under the huge dome of a 480-foot-long circus tent set up in downtown Los Angeles.

This was Graham's first crusade in Los Angeles. He had been invited by a group of local businessmen called Christ for Greater Los Angeles, which was sponsoring the crusade. They needed a good preacher to attract large crowds. For the 1949 crusade, their choice was the young, new evangelist Billy Graham. An evangelist is a preacher who spreads the news about Jesus Christ to believers and nonbelievers alike.

In 1949, Billy Graham was just one of a number of little-known evangelists in the United States.[1] Each night for four weeks, crowds in Los Angeles had come to hear this energetic young man. They sat spellbound as he stalked back and forth across the 150-foot stage. Tall and thin, with wavy blond hair and intense eyes, Graham wore pastel suits, vivid handpainted ties, and bright patterned socks.[2] In this colorful attire, Graham made an impression on his listeners' eyes as well as their hearts.

With such sermons as "Prepare to Meet Thy God" and "Judgment,"[3] Graham has described his preaching style as "loud and enthusiastic."[4] His words created a sense of urgency in the audience. He said that God's judgment was coming and that they must repent of their sins before it was too late.[5]

The Los Angeles crusade had already been extended one week longer than first planned, and Graham was pleased with its success. He wrote to a friend, "We are having by far the largest evangelistic campaign of our entire ministry."[6] Yet as the fourth week drew to a close, no huge crowds had appeared to hear Graham preach. The Christ for Greater Los Angeles Committee was ready to take down the tent and bring the crusade to an end.

This night, however, would be different. As Graham slowly trudged toward the tent, something caught his attention. Suddenly, he was surrounded by a group of reporters. With pencils and paper in hand, they shouted questions at him. Cameras flashed in his startled face as the press snapped his picture. "Reporters and cameramen [were] crawling all over the place," Graham said later.[7]

That kind of attention from the Los Angeles press was something new for Billy Graham. Up to then, the Los Angeles crusade had seen very little press coverage at all.[8] The only attention he had received was the ads the crusade committee had placed in the newspapers. By one account, most of the millions who lived in Los Angeles were not even aware of the Graham crusade.[9] But the media attention Graham received that night thrust him into the limelight. It began after William Randolph Hearst telegraphed a simple order to his newspaper editors: "Puff Graham."

To most people, those two words do not make much sense. But in the world of newspaper publishing, the command to "puff" something tells reporters to give that subject a lot of coverage.

Simply having more attention in the Los Angeles papers would have been a big boost to the crusade. But an order from William Randolph Hearst meant much more than that. Hearst was one of the most well known and powerful newspaper publishers in the country. In 1949 he controlled a chain of seventeen newspapers in cities including Boston, Chicago, New York, Detroit, and Los Angeles. If Hearst wanted a subject to get attention, it would be covered from coast to coast.

That is exactly what happened to Billy Graham. With the order "Puff Graham," Hearst's newspaper reporters went into action. One reporter told a bewildered Graham that night, "You've just been kissed by William Randolph Hearst."[10]

The next day, Hearst's morning and evening local papers, the *Los Angeles Herald* and the *Los Angeles Examiner*, featured Graham. They carried banner headlines, full stories, and pictures. Los Angeles was suddenly buzzing with excitement and interest in Graham and the crusade. One observer recalled, "The cabbies would start talking to you about Billy Graham, and waitresses and shop girls and most anyone."[11]

Twelve of Hearst's other papers across the nation quickly followed with crusade coverage. After that, *Time*, *Life*, and *Newsweek* magazines picked up the story. In an article titled "Sickle for the Harvest," *Time* magazine introduced Billy Graham to its readers. A writer described him "dominating his huge audience from the moment he strides on stage."[12] *Life* magazine proclaimed, "A New Evangelist Arises" and told of Graham's impact as "an energetic young evangelist."[13] The Associated Press, United Press International, and International News Service also picked up the story, spreading it nationwide.

Almost overnight, Graham's future changed. He became known to people throughout the United States, and his three-week crusade expanded to eight weeks. For the last three weeks, the crusade tent was packed and overflowing with listeners. Three thousand more chairs were set up, and still that was not enough. On the last evening, eleven thousand people filled the tent and spilled out into the surrounding streets two hours before the service was

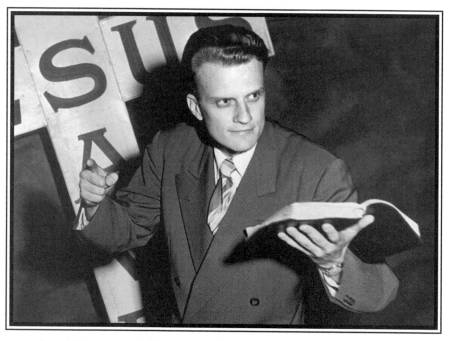

Coast-to-coast publicity about a new, "energetic young evangelist" thrust Billy Graham into the spotlight.

even scheduled to begin.[14] By the time the crusade was over, 350,000 people in Los Angeles had heard Billy Graham preach.

To this day no one can say for sure what prompted Hearst to order the Graham publicity. Some say Hearst thought Graham had a fine, moral message that would benefit the nation's youth. Others think that as a strong anti-Communist, Hearst wanted to publicize Graham's message against Communism. Perhaps Hearst simply thought coverage of Graham's crusade would interest lots of people and make them want to buy his papers.[15]

Regardless of the reason, Hearst's command, combined with Graham's energy, talent, and commitment to his ministry, would have far-reaching effects. Graham's impact in Los Angeles was just the beginning. From there, he went on to a ministry that would span the globe.

During the next fifty years, Billy Graham would preach directly to more than 100 million people. Millions more would hear his message through his best-selling books, his syndicated newspaper column, his weekly radio broadcasts, and his television crusades. Graham would also become the friend and spiritual adviser to ten United States presidents, providing spiritual counsel and advice during good times and bad. As an ambassador for Christians and for his country, Graham would visit with political and religious leaders all over the world. He would also work to promote peace in areas of unrest. With the 1949 Los Angeles Crusade, Billy Graham and his message were catapulted into a ministry that would be felt for generations to come.

Farm Boy

William Franklin Graham, Jr., or "Billy," as he was later known to his followers all over the world, was born on November 7, 1918. Named for his father, Billy was the first of four Graham children. At that time, the Grahams lived in a modest farmhouse with no running water or indoor bathrooms. The house was located on the Graham family's two-hundred-acre farm about four miles outside Charlotte, North Carolina.

Billy's father, Franklin Sr., was a quiet, hard-working man. He managed the farm with the help of his younger brother, Clyde. Besides raising dairy cows, the Grahams grew acres of corn, wheat, barley, and rye. Franklin Graham had married Morrow

Coffey in 1916, and they settled down together to run the farm and start a family.

When Billy was eighteen months old, his sister Catherine was born. Four years later, his brother Melvin arrived. Several years after that, the family moved into a larger, two-story brick house that they had built nearby to accommodate their growing family. It had white columns on the front porch and the luxury of indoor bathrooms and running water. Magnolia and oak trees shaded the front yard. Billy and Melvin shared an upstairs corner bedroom that looked out on trees behind the house.

The Graham Brothers' Farm was an ideal place for a young boy like Billy, or "Billy Frank" as he was called, to run and play. Along with the dairy cows, there were horses, chickens, dogs, and cats to occupy a growing boy's attention. He even had a pet goat that he could hitch to a little cart and drive around the farm.

Billy also had plenty of land to explore. Besides the pastures, there were woods to play in. After becoming acquainted with the Tarzan books by Edgar Rice Burroughs, Billy loved to pretend he was Tarzan, swinging from trees and mimicking Tarzan's piercing call.

The farm gave young Billy space for his excess energy. "There was never any quietness about Billy," his mother once said.[1] Far from being a well-behaved little boy, Billy's liveliness and imagination drove his parents and his siblings to distraction. "He often made their lives miserable with his teasing and tormenting," Morrow Graham later said.[2] Once he pushed a dresser out of a bedroom and down the stairs. Another time he cracked a neighbor's car windshield with his slingshot. He even fought with his younger sister, Catherine, over a can of baked beans, shoving her through two sets of swinging doors.[3]

Yet, despite his mischief-making, Billy showed a tenderness of spirit even as a boy. He was especially close to his mother. Each Sunday after church he gathered flowers from the woods around their house and presented them to his mother. "My greatest joy was to please her," he said.[4]

Franklin Graham, Sr., was devoted to his farm, his family, and his faith. Billy saw his father hard at work from before dawn until well after sunset each day. Even though his focus on farmwork kept him from hobbies like hunting or fishing, Billy's father did enjoy telling jokes and stories, as well as smoking an occasional cigar.[5]

Farm life was rigorous for Morrow Graham as well. Every morning she had breakfast on the table by 5:30 for her family and the hired farmhands. She served grits, gravy, eggs, ham or bacon, homemade rolls, and all the milk they could drink.[6] During the day, Billy's mother chopped wood for the stove, hauled water to the kitchen, and hoed the vegetable garden.

As their family grew, the Grahams created a strict and orderly household. "I was taught that laziness was one of the worst evils, and that there was dignity and honor in labor," said Billy.[7] Sometimes for a special treat on Saturday nights, Franklin Graham would drive the family into Charlotte to Nivens Drugstore. There the rest of the family would get ice cream cones or sodas (never both) while Billy's father got a shave at the barbershop. Suzie Nicholson, who helped Billy's mother with the family cooking and cleaning, sometimes sneaked penny candy to the Graham children because she thought they did not get enough sweets from their parents.[8]

Farm life required a lot of hard work from Billy, too. From the time he was six, his father would get him up as early as 3:00 o'clock each morning. Sleepily, he would stumble outside and through the alfalfa field to the barn for his first job of the day: milking the cows. Sitting on a three-legged stool and using a tin milk pail, Billy milked twenty cows each morning and twenty each afternoon after school. Each cow took about five minutes, so altogether, the job took almost two hours. After that, he carted the fresh milk across the road to his Uncle Clyde's house, where it would be poured into glass bottles, fitted with cardboard stoppers, and stamped "Graham Brothers' Dairy." Then it was delivered to customers. Billy also brought in fresh hay for the cows and shoveled manure from their stalls.

The school Billy attended was not any more successful in harnessing his excess energy than his mother was. Once, a teacher had to chase him around the desks in the school room and smack him with a ruler to settle him down.[9] He also got his start at public speaking in elementary school. His very first speech was delivered as Uncle Sam in a school pageant. Costumed in a beard and long coat, Graham has never forgotten how he felt that day: "My knees shook, my hands perspired, and I vowed to myself that I would never be a public speaker."[10]

The Grahams were like many other families in the Deep South in their tradition of strong religious faith. As he grew, Billy became aware of his parents' faith as a central theme for their family. They gathered in the den after supper each evening for daily devotions. Billy's mother read verses from the Bible. Then his father led the family in prayer, on their knees, sometimes for twenty or thirty minutes. Billy later remembered, "That was the main event of the day in our house."[11]

Each week, the Grahams drove five miles in their Model-A Ford to attend Sunday school and church at the Associated Reformed Presbyterian Church in downtown Charlotte. Looking back, Billy said, "I had to attend every worship service . . . . I secretly rebelled [against it.]."[12]

Sundays brought other problems, too. On that day, no one in the Graham household was allowed to read newspaper comics or play games. The only acceptable activity was reading from the Bible or other religious books. In the afternoon the family sat in the living room listening to Charles Fuller's *Old-Fashioned Revival Hour* on the radio. Typical of most boys his age, Billy was not happy about those restrictions on his time and activities. "I didn't like Sundays then at all," he said. "I dreaded to see them come."[13]

As Billy got older, his zest for living grew even stronger. By the time he was fourteen, he had a new little sister, Jean. He enjoyed carrying her around on his shoulders. He was tall and skinny—the tallest in

Billy grew up on a farm, where there were always plenty of chores. Prayer was an important part of his family life.

his class at school—with a ready grin. His love was baseball. He dreamed of playing in the major leagues as a first baseman one day.[14]

In high school, Billy continued to have trouble settling down to his schoolwork. "He wasn't one to let study interfere with his education," joked his mother.[15] During his last year in high school, one of his teachers visited Billy's home to tell his mother that Billy might not graduate with his class. He was smart enough; that was not the problem. He just spent his time on other interests.

Along with baseball, Billy's other interests included girls and fast cars. The girls liked Billy, too. With his wavy blond hair and deep-set blue eyes, Billy did not lack for dates. Sometimes he even had two dates in one evening. His sister Catherine said Billy was "in love with a different girl every day."[16]

Once he could drive, Billy's favorite Saturday night pleasure was to race his dad's dark blue Plymouth as fast as it would go down backcountry roads with a pretty girl at his side.[17] He got into fights from time to time, once breaking a milk bottle over an opponent's head. As a teenager, Graham says he "had a rebellious heart and mind. . . . I understood little and resented my parents, my teachers, my humdrum life as a farmhand and high-school student."[18]

When Billy was sixteen, a revival meeting came to Charlotte. Revivals were not uncommon in the South then, especially in the summer. Many who attend revivals are already members of local churches. They come to hear a good sermon and to be inspired to lead better lives. Others, who are not religious and do not belong to any church, may come out of curiosity or just for something to do. Sometimes they come to see if the preacher's message will be so moving that it will convince them to have faith in God. Many find revivals inspiring. But others think revivals are too circus-like.

At a typical revival, the evangelist, or preacher, presents to the audience the sins of their everyday lives—sins that Satan, or the Devil, uses to tempt them. These include alcohol, cursing, adultery, gambling, cheating, and lying. After that, the audience is encouraged to repent of, or be sorry for, their sins, and to accept Christ as their savior. The preacher tells them that they can live with Christ in heaven when they die. Often the preacher has a dramatic appearance and delivery. His piercing eyes, broad gestures, and loud voice engage his audience and hold people's interest.

Catering to the strong religious faith and interest in Christ's Second Coming found in the Deep South, Charlotte welcomed many revivalists. When a revival came to town, it usually lasted for several weeks, drawing many townspeople. It would be held in a hastily built building or tent called a tabernacle.

The revival that came to Charlotte in August 1934 changed Billy Graham's life. The Reverend Dr. Mordecai Ham was the evangelist who preached. The tabernacle for the revival in Charlotte was built of raw pine boards on an empty lot. Its red clay floor was topped with straw and sawdust. Under bare lightbulbs hastily strung from the overhead rafters, the townspeople gathered in the August heat with their paper fans to hear the Reverend Dr. Ham.

Billy had not intended to go to the revival at all. For one thing, he did not consider himself a very religious person. So why should he go? "I did not want anything to do with anyone called an evangelist," said Graham later.[19] But after several days, Billy's curiosity got the better of him. He heard that "Brother Ham" was preaching about the sinfulness of the high school students in Charlotte. That meant him! A friend persuaded Billy to go with him to the revival.

Listening to the Reverend Dr. Ham, Billy was caught up in the energy, emotion, and excitement of the evening. After that first night, he went back again and again. "There's a gre-a-a-a-t sinner here tonight!" Ham railed at his listeners. Billy thought the evangelist was talking directly to him. To avoid the preacher's gaze, Billy joined the choir sitting behind Brother Ham. But Ham's message had reached its mark. "His words and his way with words grabbed my mind, gripped my heart," said Graham.[20] One night, after Ham's invitation to his listeners to accept Christ, Billy Graham came forward to become a Christian.

The Call

Billy's conversion experience at Mordecai Ham's revival was not what he had expected: "I didn't have any tears, I didn't have any emotion, I didn't hear any thunder, there was no lightning. But right there, I made my decision for Christ. It was as simple as that. . . ."[1]

Billy Graham went back to Sharon High School in the fall of 1934 to begin his junior year. He did not want to be one of those people who accepted Christ one day and then went back to their old ways once the emotion of the time faded. But how should he feel? What should he do?

Although Billy's behavior did not change dramatically after his conversion, it did change in small ways. He resolved to work harder at school, be nicer to those around him, and spend more time studying the Bible.[2] For a while he also became more critical of his friends' behavior. If he saw a friend doing something that would be frowned upon in his new Christian world, Billy would point it out. That unpopular habit earned him the title of "the Preacher Boy."[3]

Billy graduated from high school on schedule in 1936, despite his teacher's earlier concern. He was one of twenty-five seniors. His commitment to his faith was still strong. In his school yearbook, Billy wrote, "My hopes and plans for the future [are] to serve God and do His will as a minister of the Gospel."[4]

With the end of high school, he was anxious to get out of Charlotte and see something of the world.[5] So he got a job for the summer as a Fuller Brush salesman. He and three friends traveled through South Carolina selling brushes to housewives door-to-door.

Every morning, the four young men, who were all faithful Christians, started the day together with prayer. Then they separated. Each spent the rest of the day trudging from house to house throughout the town, trying to persuade people to order some cleaning brushes from a suitcase of samples. "I went at it with all the zest that I could and would work from morning until night selling brushes," said Graham.[6]

Housewives were not always happy to have salesmen call. Once, a woman dumped a bucket of water on Graham when he rang her doorbell.[7] But Graham was not put off. "I was convinced that Fuller brushes were the best product money could buy, and I was dedicated to the proposition that every family ought to have Fuller brushes," he said.[8] He also began saying a little prayer as he approached each home. He did not ask God to help him make a sale. Instead, he just asked for the chance "to witness for Christ"—to share his religious beliefs. Some customers complained about his "hard sell" approach.[9]

At night the salesmen went to a boardinghouse, where they could get a room and meals for one dollar a day. They typically stayed three or four days in a town and then moved on to another. They could earn as much as $50 to $75 per week, which was an excellent income for an eighteen-year-old at that time. Billy used most of his money to add to his snappy wardrobe. He favored suits in pastel hues and wild, multicolored ties.

With his good looks, enthusiasm, and sincerity, Billy Graham was a successful salesman. By the end of the summer, he was the top-selling Fuller Brush salesman in North and South Carolina.[10] The experience brought Graham other benefits as well. He learned self-reliance by being on his own. He also learned a lot about himself, and his self-confidence grew.

Often during that summer, Graham returned home on weekends. Sometimes he would try his hand at preaching. His congregations usually consisted of jail inmates or unwed mothers. Those first attempts were less than promising, though. As with his childhood experience as Uncle Sam, Graham was awkward and uncomfortable in his delivery. Nervous and stressed, he had a distracting habit of fiddling with his coat while he spoke.[11]

As the end of the summer drew nearer, Billy Graham's plans for the future were uncertain.[12] Should he go to college? Or should he stay on the farm with his father and take over the family dairy business one day? Many expected Billy, as the older Graham son, to work the farm with his dad and uncle, and eventually take over the business. But that role would eventually fall to Melvin. Other plans were in store for Billy.

One day, one of the South's leading evangelists, Bob Jones, came to Charlotte to speak at a local high school. He was recruiting students to attend Bob Jones College, in Cleveland, Tennessee. Jones had founded the college as a place to train evangelists for the ministry. Once Morrow Graham heard Jones, she decided that was where her son Billy should go.

So in the fall of 1936, Graham headed off to Cleveland, Tennessee, to begin his studies. He was one of three hundred students at Bob Jones College. After his early enthusiasm for the school wore off, Graham was left with shock and dismay at his new environment. He knew what it was like to live in a strict Christian home. But this college was more like a jail to him! "Griping Not Tolerated" signs were posted on the dormitory room walls. Students' mail was read and checked for un-Christian ideas.

The young men and women could not even speak to one another in passing during the day. Holding hands with someone of the opposite sex was out of the question. As for dating, that was allowed only once a week. A "date" lasted for just fifteen minutes. During the date, the boy and girl were allowed only to sit across from each other and talk in a carefully supervised room. This was no place for a fun-loving guy like Billy Graham. He later said, "A military academy could not have been more strict."[13] Billy Graham was miserable.

At Christmas he went home for vacation. As things turned out, he would never resume his studies at Bob Jones College. Instead, his college roommate, Wendell Phillips, persuaded Billy to try a different school: Florida Bible Institute near Tampa, Florida. Wendell was transferring there, and he thought Billy might like it, too.

So as 1937 began, Billy headed south. Florida was new to him, and he immediately fell in love with its balmy weather, exotic flowers, and towering palm trees.[14]

The school was located in Temple Terrace, a small town fifteen miles east of Tampa. Fewer than one hundred men and women were enrolled. A former country club, the campus had tennis courts, a golf course, and Spanish-style buildings of cream-colored stucco with red-tiled roofs. Palm trees dotted the lawn in front of the main building.

Besides holding classes, the Florida Bible Institute doubled as a religious retreat center for preachers and businesspeople. The students could earn extra money by carrying luggage, caddying for golfers, waiting tables, and washing dishes. This also gave them the chance to meet evangelists and ministers from around the country who came there for rest and renewal.

Florida Bible Institute suited Billy perfectly. After his experience at Bob Jones College, he felt as if he had been released from jail.[15] Each day he and the other students took courses on prophecy, modern missions, Bible geography, hymnology, and Bible customs. They also attended daily chapel services.

In addition to their studies and part-time work, the students were expected to be ready to preach anywhere at any time. Billy Graham carefully prepared four sermons, each to last about forty-five minutes.

One day he got his chance. The dean of the school took Graham to Jacksonville, Florida, and asked him to preach at a small Baptist Church in the nearby town of Bostwick. It would be a good chance for Graham to get some practice at the pulpit. Graham began preaching his first prepared sermon to the thirty people in the congregation. To his dismay, his material did not take as long to deliver as he had expected. His nervousness made him talk too fast. The sermon he had thought would take forty-five minutes actually lasted about two minutes! So he started in with his second sermon, and then had to follow with his third and his fourth. By the time he was finished, he had preached for a grand total of eight minutes.[16]

While at the Florida Bible Institute, Graham also practiced preaching in downtown Tampa. He would stand on the streets preaching at passersby. Or he would go to bars and preach to drunks about the evils of their ways. Often he was booed or laughed at. Once

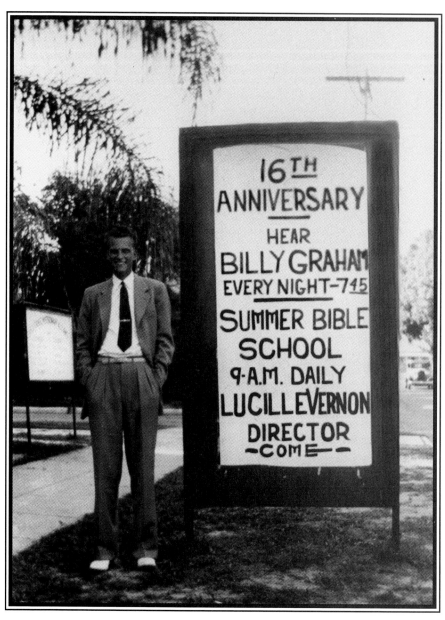

Summer Bible School gave the young preacher an opportunity to exercise his new skills.

he was even thrown into a gutter by an angry listener.[17] But that kind of punishment did not stop him. To Graham, it was an honor to suffer for his beliefs.[18]

He also practiced preaching by himself on the banks of the nearby Hillsboro River. There, to an audience of squirrels, birds, and an occasional snake, Graham began to develop his preaching style. "Any old stump along the river was a good pulpit, even if I didn't have anyone to listen to me," he said.[19]

Graham learned how to pace his sentences for the greatest effect. He also practiced using his hands and body to emphasize his message. Later he was nick-named the "Preaching Windmill" because he flailed his arms so wildly as he preached.[20]

With all his preparation for the ministry, though, Billy Graham remained unsure. Was that really what he wanted to do with his life? He was torn by indecision. He knew he was not an exceptional preacher.[21]

On a cool spring night in 1938, Billy Graham was unable to sleep as he thought about his future. He left his room and began wandering around the campus golf course. He was searching for direction. What did God want him to do? Finally, at the eighteenth hole, Graham said, "I remember getting on my knees and saying, 'Oh God, if you want me to preach, I will do it.'"[22] Suddenly, all his attention, enthusiasm, and energy had found a sure direction. He knew he would become a preacher after all.

Until this time, Billy Graham remained a member of the Presbyterian church his family attended in Charlotte. But in December of 1938, he was rebaptized, this time as a Southern Baptist. A year later he was ordained as a Baptist minister.

In the summer of 1940, Graham completed his studies at the Florida Bible Institute. He graduated with a Christian Worker's Diploma, the certificate offered by the Bible institute, which was not an accredited academic college or university. He was president of his eleven-member graduating class and editor of the yearbook.

This time, Graham knew what direction he would take next. Earlier that year, he had worked as a caddy, carrying golf clubs for a visiting Christian businessman. During his golf game, the businessman had been so impressed with Graham's enthusiasm and Christian conviction that he offered to pay for a year's expenses at Wheaton College. Wheaton was a well-respected four-year Christian college near Chicago, Illinois. Studying there would help round out and broaden Graham's education. So in the fall of 1940, Billy Graham packed his bags once again, this time heading north.

The Girl from China

Graham's move to Illinois was an eye-opening experience. Going from the rural Deep South to the Chicago area in the Midwest brought all sorts of changes. First, there was the weather. Chicago, known as "the windy city," has the hot, humid summers that Graham was used to. But the winters were a big change, with below-freezing temperatures and lots of snow and ice. Then there were the cultural differences involved in moving to a different part of the country. People spoke differently in Chicago; life moved at a faster pace. People near the big city seemed more sophisticated and experienced. And there were so many more people! Coming from the tiny Florida Bible Institute, Graham now had to make his way among one thousand students at Wheaton College.

Academically, Wheaton offered a much broader range of courses, and Graham found the demands more rigorous.[1] The students in Illinois found Billy Graham a bit of a curiosity. They were unused to hearing a southern drawl like his. His pastel suits and bright ties stood out. The fact that he was already an ordained minister with a lot of preaching experience set him apart from the other students as well. With all these changes, Graham felt uncomfortable and out of place at Wheaton at first.[2]

He decided to major in anthropology, the scientific study of human beings, their origins, and their cultures. He thought it would tie in well with his Christian studies at the Florida Bible Institute. He also hoped it would be easy.[3] Along with his studies, Graham began a job with the Wheaton College Student Trucking Service. The towing service hauled trash and moved furniture in a battered old yellow pickup truck.

Ruth McCue Bell, another student at Wheaton, had come there from China the year before. Her parents were American Christian missionaries, and she had grown up in Tsingkiangpu in northeast China. After completing high school, she had come nine thousand miles to Wheaton to finish her education. Bell's goal was to prepare herself for missionary service in Tibet. She wanted to go there as a single woman and devote her life to Christian missionary work. Unlike many young women of her time, she had no interest in finding a husband in college. In fact, finding a husband was the very thing that might prevent her dream of missionary life in Tibet.[4]

To prepare for her career, Bell was majoring in Bible studies and minoring in art. Her day began at 5:00 a.m. with Bible reading and prayer, and she had a reputation as the most devoted Christian girl on the Wheaton campus.[5] Bell had lots of friends and was well respected as a student and a Christian.[6] With hazel eyes and dark brown hair, she was also known as one of Wheaton's most beautiful coeds.

One day, while Graham was on the job lugging an overstuffed chair up the front steps of one of the campus dormitories, he crossed paths with Ruth Bell. Hot, sweaty, and dirty, he was not at his best. But he got her attention.

Bell had heard about this new student who had recently transferred from the distant South. Shortly after that first chance passing, a mutual friend introduced them. Bell was a sophomore; Graham was a freshman. It took him a month to get up his courage to ask her for a date. But finally he did. They went to a Sunday afternoon musical presentation. After the performance, they took a slow walk through the snow across Wheaton's campus for tea at a professor's house.

Graham was smitten with Ruth Bell from the beginning. "I fell in love right that minute," he later reported.[7] He also sent a letter to his mother with a glowing description of Bell, writing, "This is the girl I am going to marry."[8] As for Bell, despite her career plans she found herself praying, "God, if You let me

"I fell in love right that minute," said Graham after meeting Ruth Bell.

serve You with that man I'd consider it the greatest privilege in my life."[9]

When school was out that year, Graham asked Bell to marry him. But she was not sure. She loved Bill, as she called him. But what about her dream of being a missionary in Tibet? What did God want her to do? After several weeks of indecision and prayer, she finally wrote to Graham of her decision to accept his proposal. Even so, Bell did not look forward to life as the wife of an evangelist. Instead, she prepared herself for what she expected—a life of hardships, financial strain, and criticism from the public.[10]

On December 7, 1941, the Japanese bombed the United States naval base at Pearl Harbor in the Hawaiian Islands. Within the week America declared war on Japan and Germany. Everywhere young men were being drafted or signing up to fight in the war. Even though ministers were not required to serve in the military, Graham considered enlisting as a soldier and later as a chaplain. But to be an army chaplain he had to finish school and get one year's experience as a full-time pastor. So rather than joining the army immediately, he continued his studies at Wheaton.

In the fall of 1942, Bell left Wheaton for a semester to be with her sister, Rosa, in Albuquerque, New Mexico. Rosa was ill with tuberculosis, a serious disease that affects the lungs. While Bell was away, Graham added to his responsibilities by preaching regularly at the Western Springs Baptist Church. His preaching style developed and his confidence grew. He began getting a reputation as a fine, dynamic young evangelistic preacher.[11]

While Bell was in New Mexico, old doubts about her engagement to Graham resurfaced. When she returned to Wheaton in January 1943, she told him that she thought they should cancel their plans to marry. Thoughts of Tibet still tempted her. Perhaps they could solve the problem if he would go there with her?

Graham was not put off by her uncertainty. He asked her, "Do you believe that God brought us together?" She said she did. "In that case, God will lead me and you will do the following." And according to Bell, she has been following him ever since.[12]

With those plans settled, other plans for their future soon fell into place as well. The congregation of Western Springs Baptist Church asked Graham to be its full-time pastor once he graduated from school. He accepted.

Graham and Bell both graduated from Wheaton in June 1943. They were married later that summer, on August 13, at the Presbyterian Conference Center in Montreat, North Carolina. Bell's parents had moved to Montreat in 1940 when the war prevented their return to China. Ruth wore a handmade white satin gown. Her veil reached to the floor. Melvin Graham was his brother's best man.

Returning to Chicago from their honeymoon in the Blue Ridge Mountains, the young couple moved into a four-room furnished apartment near the church. They enjoyed themselves by taking walks in their neighborhood and visiting a nearby park. Occasionally they played golf.

Yet, as with most newlyweds, it was a time of

change for them both. Ruth was learning to cook and clean house. For meals, she leaned heavily on recipes adapted from her childhood in China. She also found that her husband was messy, leaving wet bath towels draped across the top of the bathroom door for her to put away.

Graham began his full-time work as the minister of the Western Springs Baptist Church (later renamed the Village Church). It was located about fifteen miles from Wheaton. A tiny congregation, it had about thirty-five members. They met in the basement of an unfinished building. Ruth has referred to it as the one time her husband got sidetracked from his calling as an evangelist.[13] Still, she has acknowledged that the firsthand appreciation he gained about the problems and concerns of being a minister helped him relate to pastors.

Throwing himself into his new duties, Graham organized house-to-house visits. He wanted to invite residents of Western Springs to visit his little church. His standard pitch to his congregation was "Bring your neighbors. Knock on doors. Invite people to come. We'll treat them real good."[14] Under Billy Graham's leadership, church membership began to increase.

He and one of the church members also organized the Western Suburban Professional Men's Club for local businessmen. Once a month they would meet for dinner and to listen to an evangelistic speaker. The club grew very popular, with attendance soaring to more than three hundred.

In January 1944 Graham began doing a radio

show late each Sunday night. It was broadcast live from the Western Springs basement sanctuary. Torrey Johnson, pastor of Chicago's growing Midwest Bible Church, had been in charge of the popular show. But with growing responsibilities of his own, he asked Billy Graham to take it over for him. The forty-five-minute show, called *Songs in the Night*, was broadcast on WCFL radio. It consisted of gospel hymns and a short meditation. Graham hired a popular area singer named George Beverly Shea as the show's soloist. Ruth Graham helped write the scripts. She also sat near her husband during the broadcasts, passing him notes during the hymns with suggestions on what he should say next.[15]

Back in North Carolina, Graham's parents were proud of their son and his success.[16] The broadcast signal from Chicago was not strong enough for their house radio to pick up. They would sit in their car each Sunday evening, where their son's voice came in loud and clear on the car radio.

Later, broadcasts were doubled to two each Sunday. One listener remembered her family faithfully tuning in to the program on Sunday evenings when she was a young teen. Years later, she still recalled the peacefulness and comfort the hymns conveyed to her.[17]

Under Graham's leadership the show continued its popularity. Being on the radio also boosted his reputation, which led to more invitations to speak in the area. The publicity also brought additional members to his church.

Through all his varied activities, Graham had

never given up the idea of serving as an army chaplain. By 1944, he met the army's requirements and received a commission as a second lieutenant. The next step was chaplains' training at Harvard Divinity School. But serious illness intervened with those plans. Graham came down with a severe case of mumps, which kept him in bed with a high fever for six weeks. Because of that, he could not take the chaplaincy course after all. By the time he was well, the war was coming to an end. So the army granted him a discharge.

With a new wife and new career, Graham's adult life was off to a great start. Soon he would move toward developing his career as an evangelist. It would change his life and the lives of millions all over the world.

The Sawdust Trail

In 1944 a new evangelistic movement was beginning to take hold in the American Midwest. Its focus was the nation's young people. An organization called Youth for Christ grew out of a concern that young people, especially those serving in the military at that time, should be encouraged in their Christian beliefs.

Because the United States was fighting in World War II, many young soldiers and sailors were stationed for a while in American cities. Some were on leave; others were waiting for their orders to be shipped overseas. Thousands were in the Chicago area alone. And most had lots of time and nervous energy on their hands. They needed an alternative to gambling, drinking alcohol, and getting into trouble on weekends.[1]

Torrey Johnson, who had asked Graham to take over the *Songs in the Night* radio program for him, was heavily involved in organizing Youth for Christ rallies. He was looking for a dynamic speaker who could inspire and energize a young audience in their faith. He thought of Billy Graham.

Graham accepted Johnson's invitation to speak at Chicago's first Youth for Christ rally. On May 24, 1944, a nervous, nail-biting Graham anxiously paced the floor, waiting for the rally to begin. Like most speakers, he worried that no one would show up. At the same time he was also worried about just the opposite—that lots of Chicago's young people would come to hear him and go away disappointed.[2]

That night, Graham preached to three thousand people. It was the largest crowd he had ever faced. He was not disappointed, and neither were they.[3] From then on he began speaking at Youth for Christ rallies throughout the Midwest.

At a typical Youth for Christ event, the speaker's first job was to attract a crowd. Then he would preach. To draw the largest audiences possible, a rally might include famous athletes, magicians, or ventriloquists in addition to the evangelist. One popular attraction at the time was a horse named MacArthur. He was trained to come up on stage and kneel in front of the cross. He could also tap the floor twelve times when asked how many disciples Jesus had. Graham said, "We used every modern means to catch the attention of the unconverted—and then we

Graham has described his preaching style as "loud and enthusiastic."

punched them right between the eyes with the Gospel."[4]

Graham's speaking commitments for Youth for Christ meant he was away from the Western Springs church more and more. His congregation noticed his frequent absences and began to grumble. After all, they were paying him to be their pastor.

Finally, Graham had to make up his mind. Was he a pastor with his own church, or was he an evangelist who traveled from city to city preaching? He chose to be an evangelist. It was the career he had prepared for, and it suited him and his talents perfectly. Graham resigned as pastor of the Western Springs church in 1945.

After that, his work for Youth for Christ took off. By the beginning of 1945, Graham was traveling all over the Midwest preaching at Youth for Christ rallies. In city after city, he spoke to high school and college students, civic clubs, and business groups. Often after he left, a Youth for Christ chapter would be set up in the city he had visited. During his first year with Youth for Christ, Graham logged two hundred thousand miles of travel.[5] It was the beginning of a pattern that would continue for the next fifty years.

By that time, Ruth Graham was expecting their first child. With her husband away more than half of the time, they decided to move to Montreat, North Carolina, and live with Ruth's parents. That way, Ruth would have her parents to keep her company. Ruth also began to resign herself to her life as the wife of a very busy evangelist. When asked how she handled having her husband gone so much of the time, she often said she would "rather see a little bit of him than a lot of any other man."[6]

On September 21, 1945, the Grahams' first daughter, Virginia Leftwich Graham (called GiGi), was born. Billy Graham missed the event. He had left that morning for Mobile, Alabama. Once he got word that Ruth was in labor, he hurried back to North Carolina, but GiGi was born before he arrived.

The next spring, Graham, Torrey Johnson, and four others made their first international Youth for Christ tour. In Great Britain and several European countries, they conducted youth rallies everywhere they went. In the British Isles alone, they held rallies in twenty-six cities. They preached in soccer fields, churches, and entertainment halls. Often, to save on expenses, they stayed in private homes rather than in hotels.

At that time, World War II had been over for less than a year. Graham and the others were struck by the devastation they saw everywhere they visited.[7] Rubble covered the streets, and bombed-out buildings dominated each city. Graham described Britain as "dark and grimy."[8] Food was still in short supply, and the weather was unusually cold. They often slept with their clothes on to stay warm.

The young, attractive Youth for Christ Americans embraced the Europeans they met with energy and enthusiasm. Some people were upset by their presence, considering them insensitive to the hardships Europe continued to endure. Most, however, found them a breath of hope at an otherwise dismal time.[9]

By this time, a man named Cliff Barrows had

become Graham's song leader at his rallies. Graham had met Barrows at a Bible conference in Asheville, North Carolina. As time went by, Graham continued to build a close-knit team. Besides Barrows, he added George Beverly Shea, who had also worked on *Songs in the Night* in Chicago. Shea's job was to sing a solo right before the sermon. The hymns he sang delighted his listeners and set a serious tone for Graham's message.[10]

Graham also added Grady Wilson, an old friend from high school, to his team. Wilson's job was to act as Graham's announcer. In addition, before a rally it was Wilson who organized prayer groups and helped with the preparations.

In 1947 Graham was invited back to his hometown of Charlotte, North Carolina, to conduct a two-week crusade there. This time it would be a Graham-only event, and not sponsored by Youth for Christ. He brought Barrows, Wilson, and Shea with him. It was the first time they all worked together as a team. The crusade was a huge success. They had to move their location from the Charlotte Armory to the American Legion field to handle the crowds.

Meanwhile, Graham agreed to a challenge from Dr. W. B. Riley, a minister and teacher who was president of Northwestern Schools in Minneapolis, Minnesota. Riley had started a Bible school in 1902. Later he expanded the school's course offerings to make Northwestern a liberal arts college and theological seminary.

By 1947, Riley was in his mid-eighties. He had first met Graham years before at the Florida Bible

Institute. Later Riley heard Graham preach at a Youth for Christ rally. Thinking about who would run Northwestern Schools after his death, Riley became convinced that Graham should be the next Northwestern president. That summer he asked Graham to visit him and said that he thought God was calling Graham to take over the presidency of the school.

Graham was not interested in the position. He was not an administrator; he was an evangelist. Yet under Riley's pressing request, Graham reluctantly accepted.[11] In January 1948, Graham became the youngest college president in the nation. He was twenty-nine years old. He took the job with the understanding that he would stay only until someone more qualified and less busy could be found. As things turned out, that would take four years.

In May of 1948, Graham's second daughter, Anne Morrow Graham, was born. By the fall of that year, Graham decided to leave Youth for Christ. He wanted to conduct crusades on his own. That way he could preach to all ages, not just to young people. So Graham, Barrows, Wilson, and Shea struck out together. They would work as a team for the next fifty years.

The four men became a close-knit unit, often playing pranks and practical jokes on one another. As they traveled from city to city, they sometimes behaved just like teenage campers—secretly "short-sheeting" someone's bed by folding the top sheet in half so it covered only the top half of the mattress. Once, Graham filled Wilson's new ten-gallon hat with shaving cream and gleefully watched as he put it on. Another time, they substituted mustard powder in the sleeping capsules Wilson's took for an airplane flight. Not only could he not sleep, but his throat and stomach felt like they were on fire for hours afterward.[12]

During the late 1940s in the United States, religious interest and church growth skyrocketed.[13] After World War II, many people felt a renewed sense of Christian commitment. There were a number of evangelists besides Billy Graham preaching from coast to coast to meet that need.[14]

Unfortunately, some of those evangelists did not always lead their lives by the rules they preached. Some got into trouble pocketing money that had been collected for the church work. Others became entranced with their near-celebrity status and became involved in improper sexual affairs. When a few evangelists got into trouble, it was easy for people to become suspicious of all evangelists.

Graham and his team did not want to be saddled with that kind of stereotype. In late 1948, while in Modesto, California, Graham, Shea, Wilson, and Barrows made a pact. They called it the Modesto Manifesto. In their agreement, they developed a code of behavior that they all agreed to follow. Their pact would keep them out of trouble and above suspicion from the public.

As Graham continued to preach to more and more people, he also began to have questions about his beliefs. The issue that especially bothered him was the question of whether he believed everything in the

Bible was completely factual. Graham's education at Bob Jones College and the Florida Bible Institute had trained him to accept the whole Bible as accurate. Yet many other Christian ministers and Bible scholars thought differently. For example, many wondered if the world really could have been created in seven days. Did God really begin human life by creating Adam and Eve, as told in the Bible? Or did humans evolve from lower life forms over millions of years, as taught by modern science? There were many stories in the Bible that defied scientific explanation or common sense. Graham was concerned. If he was questioning one part of the Bible, how could he say that *any* of it was true?

Graham was confused and upset. If he could not settle this soon, he felt he could not continue preaching.[15] He began to pray for guidance from God. He also spent a lot of time studying the Bible.

Finally, at a student conference at Forest Home, California, his indecision came to an end. After praying continually to God to help him with his uncertainty, he finally felt a sense of peace. With new confidence, Graham prayed, "Lord, I don't understand everything in this book. There are things I just cannot reconcile, that I am going to accept . . . as your . . . word by faith."[16] Once his mind was at ease, he never worried about the issue again.[17]

Armed with new confidence, Graham turned toward the event that would catapult him to national celebrity—the Los Angeles crusade.

"The Bible Says . . . !"

The Los Angeles crusade was Graham's biggest effort yet. His team began preparing for it nine months in advance.[1] Hundreds of prayer groups were organized to pray for the crusade's success. On top of that, three hundred volunteers were recruited to work as assistants during the event. Church choirs and singing groups in the Los Angeles area agreed to provide music at the services. The Christ for Greater Los Angeles Committee spent $25,000 at Graham's request to advertise the crusade.

The Los Angeles crusade was held downtown on a vacant lot at the corner of Hill Street and Washington Boulevard. A huge, three-spired circus tent was erected there to hold the hoped-for crowds. Inside the tent, nicknamed the "canvas cathedral," six thousand chairs were set up. A battery of searchlights created a "steeple of light" over the speaker's platform.[2] On the outside of the tent, a giant banner announced, "Something's Happening Inside." Alongside, Graham's face was painted in bright, circus-like colors, his intense eyes fixed on the passersby below.[3]

As the opening day loomed, Graham was nervous.[4] Perhaps he had been too optimistic about his chances for success in Los Angeles. After all, his previous crusade in Baltimore, Maryland, had been held in a theater that seated just 2,800 people. And it had been filled for only one night—the last.[5] Now six thousand seats were waiting. What if this crusade turned out to be a flop?

The Los Angeles crusade began on September 25, 1949. By the time it was over, Graham was an overnight celebrity. It was a frightening sensation for him: "What I said was being quoted all of a sudden and I knew I wasn't really all that qualified. I didn't really have the experience yet to say the right things, but the people expected me to speak with that authority. I was just scared to death. . . ."[6] Yet, with the publicity and national attention that resulted from that crusade, it seemed to Graham and his wife that surely this was what God wanted him to do.[7]

During the Los Angeles crusade, Graham's signature style became well known. With Bible in hand, he would loosen the top button of his shirt collar and begin to speak. As he continued, he grew increasingly animated, often making sweeping, dramatic gestures with his long arms. Or he would clench his fists tightly in the air to help drive home a point. One article described him "flailing his arms, crouching and pointing, coiling his big frame around the Bible he read from," and keeping his audience on the edge of their seats.[8]

As he preached, Graham paced from one end of the stage to the other. Some have calculated that he walked at least one mile during a sermon.[9] While some listeners found it distracting, it helped most keep their attention focused on him.

Throughout Graham's sermons, he would glare intently at the crowd. He locked eyes with person after person, as if he were speaking to each one individually. "If we're not guilty of one thing we're guilty of another!" he would rail. "'Thou shalt not murder'—so you say you haven't. But there are hundreds of husbands . . . who are *killing their wives by neglect. . . . You are guilty of murder!*"[10]

Graham's powerful voice, starting from a whisper and building to a blast for emphasis, held most in the audience spellbound. He has described his own impact: "I've learned to speak straight at [the audience]. I can look straight at them and I can tell when a man way back in the auditorium blinks his eyes. When he does that, I know it's time for a change of pace."[11]

Graham also made sure his message was centered firmly in the words of the Bible. Beginning sentence after sentence with the phrase "The Bible says . . . ," Graham would go on to read Scripture and proclaim his message. He wanted to tell his listeners that the words he spoke were God's words—not his own.

Graham's sermons had the same basic theme. He preached understanding and acceptance of the basic principles of Christianity. He said that all people are sinful and doomed to death and destruction. He told his listeners that God loves all people, and his son, Jesus Christ, took their punishment through his violent death. Christianity says that all those who believe in Jesus Christ will be saved from destruction and enjoy eternal life.

At the end of his sermons, Graham always closed with an invitation to come forward. "I'm going to ask you to get up out of your seat and come and stand here in front of the platform, and say by your coming, 'Tonight, I want Christ in my heart,'" he would encourage the crowd.[12] Then he would bow his head silently, and the choir would begin singing an old Gospel hymn as people slowly rose from their chairs and came forward.

After his groundbreaking crusade in Los Angeles, Graham headed across the country to Boston, Massachusetts. At first he booked just one service for New Year's Eve. But it soon expanded to an eighteen-day engagement. Even without much advance preparation or publicity, Graham once again drew crowds that surprised him. He was thrilled. Yet at the same time he was terrified. He said it was God's power that brought the crowds to him. He was convinced that if he ever took personal credit for his popularity, his success would abruptly end.[13]

Graham's next crusade was held in Columbia, South Carolina. A *Life* magazine article described the revival as "spellbinding."[14] His listeners responded by overflowing the University of South Carolina stadium. At forty-two thousand, it was the largest crowd Graham had ever drawn.

In one of his sermons there, Graham described heaven as a place with golden streets and beautiful pearl gates. Fruit trees would produce different kinds of fruit during the heavenly year. On the other hand, he said, hell was "so horrible that it cannot be expressed in the language of man."[15] He also warned his listeners that at Judgment Day, God would review each person's life in detail, because "God has had His television cameras on you."[16]

From South Carolina, Graham and his team headed north into New England. In twenty-eight days, they held a whirlwind of crusades in sixteen cities. The tour ended in Boston, with fifty thousand people gathering outdoors in Boston Common in the pouring rain to hear Graham preach. Then, shortly before he began his sermon, the sun broke through and the rain stopped.

In July 1950, Graham and his team were in Portland, Oregon, for a six-week engagement. To prepare for the crowds, a twelve-thousand-seat tabernacle was built for the event. Even so, the first service was standing room only. More than twenty thousand people showed up to hear him. By the time it was over, more than a half million people had attended the six-week Graham crusade.

While he was in Portland, Graham was approached about doing a weekly radio show. In 1950, radio was still the communication technology of choice in most homes. Television had been invented

Fifty thousand people crowded historic Boston Common in 1950 to hear the fiery evangelist.

in 1923, but it was not yet common in American homes. Graham was offered a contract with the American Broadcasting Company that would put him on national radio. The first live broadcast would take place from his upcoming crusade in Atlanta, Georgia.

Graham also began to realize he needed a way to handle all the money he was receiving in donations. He wanted to make sure that the funds were managed in such a way that no one could criticize him or his team. He wanted people to know that when they contributed to his organization, it went to help others rather than to make him rich. He set up a nonprofit organization called the Billy Graham Evangelistic

Association (BGEA). Headquartered in Minneapolis, Minnesota, the BGEA also began to handle the ever-increasing mail that Graham was receiving from his listeners.

Another beginning came from the crusade in Portland. One of his crusades had been filmed and became a color documentary called *The Portland Story*. It would be used to publicize his work to potential sponsors. The film was produced by Great Commission Films, which eventually merged with Billy Graham Films to become World Wide Pictures. After that first effort, Graham produced a steady stream of more than two hundred documentaries of his crusades as well as fictional films about people turning to Jesus Christ.

On November 5, 1950, in Atlanta, Georgia, Graham broadcast the first of his weekly radio shows, *The Hour of Decision*. The thirty-minute program would air at two o'clock on Sunday afternoons. Each *Hour of Decision* show opened to the music of "The Battle Hymn of the Republic." Then came the announcement, "Each week at this time . . . for *you* . . . for the *nation* . . . *this* is the *Hour of Decision!*"[17] Then Grady Wilson would read a passage from the Bible, followed by Shea singing a hymn. Next, Graham would present his message. Often he would relate current events to the Bible, guiding his listeners to his view that eternal hell was at hand for those who did not repent of their sins and turn to God.

The Hour of Decision was an immediate hit. Within five weeks it had the greatest number of listeners ever for a religious broadcast.[18] The show started out on

The first live broadcast of Graham's radio show, The Hour of Decision, *came from Atlanta, Georgia.*

150 stations, but in years to come it would be heard on more than 1,000 stations across the country.

Despite Graham's efforts to keep his finances above criticism, trouble hounded him in Atlanta. The *Atlanta Constitution* published an unflattering article on December 11, 1950, entitled "Graham's 'Love Offering' Collected at Final Service." A picture with the article showed smiling ushers holding up four large bags filled with money. Worse, the picture and article were printed in newspapers across the country. After that, Graham had the Billy Graham Evangelistic Association put him on its payroll. He would earn a set salary from then on, no matter how much money the organization collected.

The arrival of Graham's third daughter closed out the year. Ruth Bell Graham, whom they would call Bunny, was born in December 1950.

In early 1952, Graham resigned as president of Northwestern Schools. Although it was a sidetrack from his true vocation, the opportunity had given him experience in managing an organization and its finances. He also came away with a greater understanding of young people. Yet, he knew evangelism was his true work.

Building on Success

At the start of 1952, Graham and his team began their first crusade in Washington, D.C. It would last five weeks and attract a lot of attention from the nation's lawmakers. Many senators and representatives came to hear Graham preach, with as many as fifty attending a single meeting.[1] While in Washington, Graham also got the chance to meet many of the nation's leaders. Several, including Richard M. Nixon and Lyndon B. Johnson, would become his lifelong friends.

Graham was given special permission by Congress to hold a service on the steps of the Capitol. It was the first time a formal religious service had been held there. Even though the weather was cold and rainy that day, forty thousand people gathered to hear Graham preach.[2]

In 1952, Graham preached from the steps of the Capitol in Washington, D.C.

Several months after the Washington crusade, Graham's fourth child—and first son—was born. He and Ruth named their new baby William Franklin Graham III.

Later in 1952, Graham decided to begin writing a newspaper column. By this time he was receiving thousands of requests for personal and spiritual advice from people everywhere. It was impossible for him to keep up with the volume of individual letters, so he decided on a broader response through the newspaper. His new daily column, called "My Answer," appeared for the first time in December 1952. Each day, Graham gave his views and advice.

He wrote on everything from how to have a happy marriage and how to raise children, to living a Christian life and how to find God. The column was a big hit. By the end of the next year it was carried by seventy-three newspapers across the country, reaching as many as 15 million readers.[3]

At Christmastime in 1952 Graham made a trip to South Korea. The United States was in the middle of an undeclared war there, trying to keep South Korea from being taken over by the Communists of North Korea and China. Graham had received a number of letters from servicemen and chaplains who thought that a visit by Graham would encourage the troops.

While in South Korea, Graham traveled all over the war-torn country preaching to civilians and soldiers alike. In military transportation, sometimes dodging snipers' bullets, he traveled to the front lines. There, Graham preached to the troops with the sound of gunfire nearby. The danger did not seem to bother him. He said, "The more dangerous it was, the more I sometimes felt I was really doing something for the Lord."[4]

Graham was shocked by the sight of soldiers physically ravaged by the war. He visited wounded soldiers in hospitals wherever he could, hoping his presence would provide some encouragement and hope. One man he talked with had been paralyzed by a bullet in his spine. The man had to lie face down in his bed, but he wanted to see Graham's face. With his eyes filled with tears, Graham quietly lay on his back underneath the young man's bed. Together they softly talked and prayed.[5]

Graham offered hope and encouragement to U.S. troops in war-torn South Korea.

Back in the United States, as Graham continued his crusades, he began to notice something that disturbed him. Although whites and blacks were both attending his services, their seating arrangements were separate. Graham's background growing up in the South had prepared him for that kind of separation. In his heart, though, he felt it was wrong. "When Christ came into my heart, people of all colors became the same, because I was seeing them through His eyes," he said.[6]

After study, thought, and prayer, Graham made a decision. Beginning in 1953, with a crusade in Chattanooga, Tennessee, Graham removed the ropes that separated the seating sections by race. No longer would that kind of discrimination be a part of his crusades. In future crusades, despite protests from local planners or predictions of trouble, Graham stuck to his convictions. "Where men are standing at the foot of the Cross, there are no racial barriers," he said. "We must dare to obey the commandment of love, and leave the consequences in [God's] hands."[7]

That year, Graham published *Peace with God*. He wrote this book because he felt ordinary people needed a book that would explain Christianity in a simple way. He and Ruth worked together on the project. The book was an immediate success, selling 125,000 copies in the first three months of its release. Millions more copies have been sold all over the world since then, and the book has been translated into fifty languages.

The next year held a new challenge for Graham. His three-month Greater London Crusade was scheduled for March through May 1954. Despite Graham's extensive preparation and high hopes for success, the event began disastrously. As he and Ruth sailed on the ocean liner S.S. *United States* toward England, they were completely unaware that trouble was brewing.

Shortly before their scheduled docking in England, Graham received a telegram warning him of a serious problem. The Billy Graham Evangelistic Association office in Minneapolis had printed a calendar to publicize the London crusade. On the calendar, it said, "What Hitler's bombs could not do, Socialism, with its accompanying evils, shortly accomplished." Socialism was a popular political movement within Great Britain. It seemed as if

As Ruth and Billy Graham sailed for England, they did not know that trouble was brewing for the evangelist.

Graham were insulting the British government and trying to interfere with politics.

Realizing the reference to socialism would offend the British, the BGEA office had already changed the word to "secularism," meaning a lack of religion. They reprinted the calendar, but a copy of the original version had made its way to London. It fell into the hands of the press, which quickly became hostile toward Graham.

As the ocean liner approached its landing at Southampton, a tugboat crowded with twenty-five reporters and eleven photographers headed out to meet the ship. Ruth Graham wrote her parents, "I knew they were after Bill's scalp."[8] Just as in Los Angeles, the Grahams were surrounded by shouting reporters and the flash of cameras. But this time the press was not friendly. Reporters were furious with Graham and wanted to discredit him in their reports.

The Grahams were immediately hit with angry questions and warnings such as, "Who invited you here, anyway?" and, "Apologize—or stay away!"[9] Graham, with a smiling Ruth by his side, calmly addressed the situation. He explained that the word "Socialism" had been a misprint. He apologized, then charmed his critics with sensitive answers to their questions. Best of all, he held a press conference later for one hundred reporters. He assured them, "I am here because I was invited to come. I'm not going to preach anti-communism, anti-socialism or anti-liberalism. . . . I have come to preach Christ."[10] By the time he was finished, the hostile crowd had calmed down. One British reporter wrote, "He seems to have a sincerity, . . . the sort of simple charm that is the greatest fun about Americans."[11]

By the time the Grahams left Southampton and arrived at Waterloo Station in London, thousands of Londoners had gathered to greet their train.[12] They were welcomed with cheers and welcoming cries of "God bless you!"

The crusade's opening night was a roller coaster of emotion for the Grahams. The services would be held in Harringay Arena in North London. It had twelve thousand seats. With all the negative publicity, no one was sure what kind of attendance to expect at the cavernous arena. In addition, the weather was bad. It was March 1, 1954, and a steady rain had turned to sleet. Who would want to go out in that kind of weather?

As the Grahams got into a car to go to the arena, they received the disappointing news that the audience there numbered only about two thousand people. That was a pitiful showing for Graham. He also knew that about three hundred reporters were there. They were just waiting to report on the embarrassing turnout in the newspapers the next day. During the unsettling eight-mile ride, said Graham, "I thought of the gloating stories that they would write. . . . We just tried to prepare our hearts to face whatever God had planned."[13]

To the Grahams' astonishment, by the time they reached the arena, the situation had improved dramatically. Thousands of people had poured from London's subway into Harringay. The arena was filled.

By the end of Graham's first week in London, Harringay was typically jammed an hour before the service was to begin. During Graham's three months there, every seat was filled. Sometimes so many people were waiting to get in that a second service had to be hastily set up to follow the first. In addition, the services were broadcast by telephone lines to 405 halls and churches throughout Great Britain.

Once the London crusade began, the Grahams were in the newspaper headlines almost daily.[14] In addition to nightly sermons, Graham was flooded with invitations to speak during the day. He and Ruth also attended parties and receptions in their honor and were given special tours of the city and its museums and attractions.

Ruth had planned to stay with her husband in London for only the first month of the crusade. That seemed like a long time to be away from her four young children. But as her departure date approached, Graham said he needed her to stay. Half jokingly, he told his staff, "If you get her the ticket [home], you're fired."[15]

For the next two months, Ruth constantly had to resist the temptation to pack up and go home. She felt useless in London.[16] Racked with indecision, she finally made up her mind. "If Bill feels he needs me— if I can in any way be of help over here—perhaps I should stay."[17] She stayed with her husband through the entire crusade.

The final meetings for the London crusade had to be scheduled in the two largest stadiums the city had to offer—Wembley and White City. On that day,

During Graham's three-month crusade in London, Harringay Arena was jammed every night.

Graham preached to crowds estimated at more than two hundred thousand people. It was the largest religious gathering in British history.[18]

By the time the three-month crusade was over, more than 2 million people had heard Billy Graham preach in London. Even the critical British press had changed its opinion of him, reporting on Graham's sincerity, openness, and integrity.[19]

But the crusade had taken its toll. Graham had lost fifteen pounds from his lanky frame, and the dark circles under his eyes had deepened dramatically. Yet, with this London success behind him, Graham's stature as an international evangelist was set.

Before he left London, Graham received an invitation from the prime minister, Sir Winston Churchill. He had been so impressed with Graham's popularity and success that he wanted to meet the young evangelist. The two men met privately at 10 Downing Street, the prime minister's residence. Churchill congratulated Graham on his crusade. They also discussed Churchill's bleak view of the world situation and Graham's hope for the future.[20]

Leaving Great Britain, Graham said, "We have fallen in love with the British people, and I trust that one of the by-products of this campaign has been the betterment of Anglo-American relations."[21] *Newsweek* magazine reported that British reaction was equally warm. An article noted the British appreciation for Graham's "charm, sincerity, and simplicity."[22]

Graham said of the campaign, "You know why God blessed the meetings in London. It wasn't great organization. It certainly wasn't great preaching. It was because millions of people around the world banded themselves to pray."[23] By October 1954, Graham's international fame had earned him a place on the cover of *Time* magazine.[24]

On Easter Sunday, 1955, Graham was back in London with a much smaller congregation. He met with Queen Elizabeth II and her husband, the Duke of Edinburgh, who invited him to preach at the Royal Chapel at Windsor Castle. Afterward, Graham had lunch with the queen. It was a fitting symbol of the success he had found in Great Britain.

Glory in
the Mountains

By the mid-1950s, Billy Graham was becoming known all over the world. Because of his growing fame, he and Ruth needed seclusion for their family, away from the prying eyes of publicity seekers. Many people knew that the Grahams lived in Montreat, North Carolina. As home of a national Presbyterian Conference Center, the town already drew a steady stream of religious pilgrims. Visitors to the little town also wanted to see where the famous evangelist and his family lived.

As people tried to steal a glimpse of Graham, his home, and his family, Ruth's flower beds were often trampled. To her amazement, she also discovered that tourists would grab any kind of memento from their yard, including stones, sticks, and leaves. Even splinters from the fence disappeared.[1] Sometimes strangers stood in the front yard and called to family members to come out and have their picture taken. It was not unusual to see someone peering into their windows at any hour of the day and night.

Once, Ruth noticed that Bunny seemed to have more money than her allowance would suggest. To her dismay, she discovered that Bunny was charging tourists who wanted to take her picture. Not to be outdone, GiGi also tried a scheme of her own for a short time, collecting a dollar from each car that passed their house.[2]

It was rare for Graham himself to be at home to fight off inquisitive tourists. But when he was, he sometimes crawled on all fours in his study from his desk to the door to avoid drawing attention from outside onlookers.

With all the attention from the public, the Grahams decided to move to a more secluded spot. When the chance arose to buy two hundred undeveloped acres close by for a reasonable price, they snapped it up. At the top of a mountain, the land was covered with apple, pear, cherry, and black walnut trees, along with rhododendron, mountain laurel, and wildflowers.

Ruth Graham began designing the house that would be her family's permanent home. She wanted a rustic structure that would settle comfortably into its untamed natural surroundings. She wanted it to be built from old materials found in the area. Soon she was seen driving through the countryside of western

Bunny looked sad as her parents kissed good-bye once again: Her father was often gone for months at a time.

North Carolina in her red Jeep. She was looking for old, abandoned cabins with materials that fit her design. She also left her telephone number at gas stations she passed along her way, in case anyone heard of cabins for sale. She bought them and had them disassembled, with the materials carted to the building site.

Under Ruth's direction, the large U-shaped house began to take shape. The planks from the old cabins became the walls of the new home. Bricks from a demolished schoolhouse covered the floors in the living room and porch, and in a glassed-in hallway connecting two wings of the house. Ruth directed most of the building because Graham was out of town so much. "I remember he told me that we could have two fireplaces. So as soon as he left [on his next trip], I told the workmen, 'Build fireplaces! Build them faster than you ever have in your life. I want five before he gets back.'"[3]

In the living room, the fireplace mantel was created from an old diving board from a nearby lake. Ruth had retrieved it from the town dump and had it carved with the German words "*Eine Feste Burg Ist Unser Gott*," meaning, "A Mighty Fortress Is Our God."

They built a split-rail fence around the yard from leftover timber. When their new home was finished, they christened it "Little Piney Cove." It could be reached only by a narrow road that wound steeply up the mountain. In this remote location, the Grahams found that most of their privacy problems had been solved.

Billy Graham loved their new home. After spending

a spring there with his family, he wrote, "I have come to love this mountaintop and would like nothing better than . . . [to] stay here for the rest of my life."[4]

During the infrequent times he was home, Graham loved being with his wife and children. The children also got glimpses into their father's personality. Just as he was quick to make dire predictions in his sermons about the consequences of falling from God's favor, Graham's around-the-house behavior revealed the concerns of a safety-conscious dad: He was a constant worrier. His family nicknamed him "Puddleglum," after a notoriously pessimistic character in *The Silver Chair* by C. S. Lewis.[5]

Ruth has described her husband as "highly disciplined, [driving himself] unmercifully."[6] He was often preoccupied with his work and crowded schedule while he was at home. One day, when Ruth was planning a dinner party menu, she asked for her husband's advice. Realizing that his mind was not with her, she decided to have some fun and see just how preoccupied he was.

"I thought we'd start off with tadpole soup," she suggested.

"Uh-huh," came Bill's distant response.

"And there is some lovely poison ivy growing in the next cove which would make a delightful salad."

"Uh-huh."

"For the main dish, I could try roasting some of those wharf rats we've been seeing around the smokehouse lately, and serve them with boiled crabgrass and baked birdseed."

"Uh-huh."

"And for dessert we could have mud soufflé. . . ." Her voice trailed off for a moment, as Bill finally came into focus.

"What was that you said about wharf rats?" he suddenly asked.[7]

At first, Ruth suffered terrible loneliness with her husband's long absences. Sometimes she even took his tweed jacket to bed with her for company.[8] As time passed, Ruth accepted that her life as the wife of an evangelist would be filled with good-byes.

By then, though, Ruth was busy with their four children. Often she felt overwhelmed and confused.[9] As in any family, she said, there were times of "terrible fighting among the children," which dismayed and upset her.[10] To combat her loneliness and the pressures of feeling like a single parent, Ruth spent hours each day poring over the Bible and other devotional materials. "The Bible stayed open in my kitchen all day. Whenever there was a spare minute, I grabbed that minute and spent it with the Bible," she said.[11]

The children missed their father, too. Once, seeing an airplane overhead flying off into the distance, one of the children, then five years old, began waving and calling, "Bye, Daddy! Bye, Daddy!"[12] There were times when Ruth took their young children to see their famous father during a crusade, and they did not recognize one another.[13] Franklin remembers coming into his parents' bedroom one morning after his father had been away on a lengthy crusade. Not recognizing his father, who had returned late the previous night, Franklin startled his parents by asking his mother about the strange man in bed with her.[14]

For his part, Graham regretted all the family time he missed. In his autobiography, he reflected, "Ruth says those of us who were off traveling missed the best part of our lives—enjoying the children as they grew. For myself, as I look back, I now know that I came through those years much the poorer both psychologically and emotionally. I missed so much by not being home to see the children grow and develop."[15]

In 1956, a longtime dream of Graham's became a reality. For several years he had wanted to create a magazine for evangelical ministers. Its purpose would be to give evangelical Christianity respect among religious intellectuals. To make this dream a reality, Graham spearheaded the effort to raise funds for the magazine and pull together the leadership it would need. His vision resulted in the magazine *Christianity Today*. The first issue appeared in November 1956.

After his success in Great Britain, Graham looked for another place to take his religious message. He became interested in conducting a crusade in India. As the plans developed, Graham was confronted with his usual precrusade fears. Christians were a small minority in India. Most people there were of the Hindu faith. A Christian crusade in India could easily be a big flop. Or, it could possibly become a turning point in the history of Indian Christianity. Graham was determined to give it a try.

Before heading to India, Graham was briefed by U.S. Secretary of State John Foster Dulles. Graham wanted to understand United States foreign policy in

Graham had long been fascinated by India, with its multicultural population and many religions. He decided to take his crusade there in 1956.

that part of the world. Then, when faced with reporters' questions, he would be less likely to accidentally say something that went against his country's foreign policy.

Graham was struck by India's exotic beauty, but the poverty and disease tore at his heart.[16] The crusade got off to an unfortunate start when his first major rally in Bombay had to be canceled. The city was in the middle of riots caused by political upheaval.

In Madras, Graham found huge crowds waiting to hear him preach. He had to use two interpreters to communicate with the people. One spoke Telugu and one spoke Tamil.[17] In just three days in Madras, Graham spoke to more than one hundred thousand people. He was amazed at the crowds and at the number of people who came forward to profess their faith. As he described the scene, he said, "All you could hear was just the tramp, tramp, tramp of bare feet and sandaled feet as they were coming forward."[18]

The climax of the India crusade was in Kottyam. There was no place big enough for Graham to preach there, so the citizens had built an amphitheater for the event, carving hundreds of terraces into a hillside by hand. The amphitheater was large enough to seat more than one hundred thousand people.

Beginning at 4:00 a.m. the day of the first scheduled service, thousands of Indians dressed in white came streaming into Kottyam to hear the American preacher. Many walked ten miles through the rain forest to get there. Some had walked fifty or sixty miles from their homes. By evening, more than seventy-five thousand people were sitting in the new amphitheater awaiting Graham's message. Graham told them, "Many Indians seem to have the idea that Christianity is a western religion. That is wrong. There were Christian churches in India before America was discovered."[19]

Before leaving India, Graham visited with Prime Minister Jawaharlal Nehru. The interview began awkwardly. Despite Graham's repeated attempts to begin conversation, Nehru remained silent. Finally, Graham launched into an explanation of his faith in Jesus Christ. With that, Nehru opened up. He had many questions and comments about Christianity in India. The two men spoke for thirty-five minutes.[20]

Graham was struck by his success in India. It seemed that regardless of the country he visited or the culture he faced, he was overwhelmed by the interest and response to his message.[21]

The next year, 1957, Graham faced his biggest challenge yet. He turned his sights on his own country—on New York City. It had long been a dream of Graham's to hold a crusade there. But up until now, he did not believe he had enough support for a New York City crusade from the local Christian community.[22] Finally, the doors were opened for Graham. He was invited by the city's Protestant Council. Fifteen hundred of its churches were eager for a visit from Graham. He could not refuse. "We need a spiritual revolution in America, and the place where it could begin is New York City," he proclaimed.[23]

Preparation for the Graham crusade in New York began eighteen months in advance.[24] By the start of the crusade, volunteers were armed with 40,000 bumper stickers, 250,000 crusade songbooks, 100,000 copies of the Gospel of John, 35,000 window posters, and 650 billboards. In addition, 110,000 people in the United States, and 160,000 in forty-eight countries prayed around the clock for the crusade's success.[25]

Before the New York crusade, Graham faced his usual case of the jitters. "We [feel] that our . . . crusade could . . . only make a dent in New York City. If I knew what I had to go through there I would probably flee with terror. But if the city can be reached, God will do it," he said in an interview.[26]

The New York crusade was scheduled to last six weeks. It began on May 15, 1957, and was held in Madison Square Garden. Graham invited Martin Luther King, Jr., to open the first meeting with prayer. Along with Graham and King, a fifteen-hundred-voice choir filled the stage.

At Madison Square Garden, where many concerts and sporting events are held, the usual blue haze of cigarette smoke was gone during Billy Graham's

"We have not come to put on a show or an entertainment," said Billy Graham in New York City. His crusade filled the huge arena that usually hosted concerts and sporting events.

crusade. Cardboard signs covered the concession stand advertisements for beer. A coat check room was temporarily transformed into a store selling Bibles and other religious materials.

The arena was filled to capacity almost every night. Overflow crowds spilled from the doorways and out into the streets. Graham cautioned, "We have not come to put on a show or an entertainment. We believe that there are many people here tonight that have hungry hearts . . . ."[27] He preached the same theme as always: "[God] is not a jolly fellow like Santa Clause. He is a Great Bookkeeper. And he is keeping book on you!"[28]

Always one to use the power of the media to his advantage, Graham also made time for interviews and guest appearances on television and radio while in New York. Then, on June 1, 1957, Graham became the nation's first televangelist. Each Saturday night his crusade was broadcast live from coast to coast by ABC-TV. The network gave the crusade one hour of prime time for each show. Graham was broadcast at the same time as shows with two popular television celebrities of the day, Jackie Gleason and Perry Como. Despite the stiff competition, approximately 96 million people viewed at least one of the seventeen televised crusades.

As the summer wore on, the New York crusade drew to a close. To hold the largest possible crowd for his last scheduled meeting in the city, the crusade was held in Yankee Stadium. That day, July 20, 1957, was the hottest day of the summer in New York City, with the temperature peaking at 105 degrees

As Graham prepared to speak from the baseball diamond in Yankee Stadium, tears of emotion filled his eyes.

Fahrenheit. Graham was expecting forty thousand to fifty thousand people. As he walked out onto the baseball diamond to begin the service, tears welled up, blocking the scene from his view for a moment. One hundred thousand people filled the stadium, a record crowd there.[29] Thousands more were outside, trying to get in and find a place to stand.

Graham decided to hold one final service before he left New York—in Times Square. As a well-known symbol of the city, Times Square was a fitting place to close the wildly successful crusade. Some 120,000 people filled Times Square that day to hear Graham. "This is the spot that thousands of tourists think of as

New York. . . . Tonight, for a few moments, it is being turned into a great cathedral," he proclaimed.[30]

By the time the New York crusade was over, more than 2.3 million people had heard Graham preach. He had also given New York sixty thousand "spiritual babies," or people who had come forward to profess their faith during one of his services. An additional result for the city, reported in *Look* magazine, was a newfound sense of comfort in talking publicly about religious beliefs among the people of the city. The article cited one of New York's leading citizens saying, "I have never known a time in New York when it seemed so natural and easy to discuss Christ and the Christian way of life."[31] The price for Graham was that he was a physical wreck. He lost thirty pounds during his four months in New York and was completely exhausted by the time the crusade was over.[32]

Into All the World

In January 1958, the Grahams' fifth child, Nelson Edman ("Ned"), was born. Billy Graham was working harder than ever. Invitations for Graham to conduct crusades poured in from all over the world. Each was evaluated at the Billy Graham Evangelistic Association, which considered the community's needs, the amount of local interest, and the kinds of meeting facilities available. The final decision about a crusade was then made by Graham himself.

Year by year, he continued to crisscross the globe. In 1960, Graham went to Africa with a crusade he called a "Safari for Souls."[1] For three months he made his way around the African continent, traveling more than fourteen thousand miles. From giant stadiums to tiny gatherings in the bush, Graham preached Christianity to all who would listen.

Graham was called "the man with his skin peeled off," by some amazed African tribesmen, and his presence even attracted some Muslim listeners.[2] Islam is the most common religion in Africa, and many Muslims were angry about Graham's visit. He preached to a third of a million Africans on his trip there, using interpreters everywhere he went.[3] His message was translated into Swahili and Linyaruanda. He saw a wide variety of audiences, from tribal dancers in Tanganyika, to Ghanaians in flaming togas and women with a Bible in one hand and an infant in the other.[4]

For all his services in Africa, Graham insisted on his longtime policy of integrated gatherings. He refused to speak in places that demanded that the races be separated. In Rhodesia (now Zimbabwe), Graham preached to an integrated audience; this was a historical first for a public meeting in the Federation of Rhodesia and Nyasaland. Because of his stance against segregation, Graham did not go to the Union of South Africa in 1960, because of its long-standing policy of apartheid (racial separation).

After the African crusade was over, Graham evaluated its effects. "Honestly, the results of this trip greatly exceeded our expectations. We had estimated that the largest crowd we'd get would be fifteen thousand. But in Lagos we must have had fifty thousand and some say one hundred thousand. Christianity has one of its greatest opportunities in Africa."[5]

In 1960, Graham began another Christian

magazine. This one, called *Decision*, was aimed at ordinary Christians, not just evangelical ministers. It included news of his crusades, a calendar of his upcoming schedule, and articles of information and inspiration. By 1970, the magazine's circulation had grown to more than four million subscribers.

In 1967, Graham got the opportunity to preach Christianity in another place that was not used to hearing evangelical Christians: Yugoslavia. He had been praying since 1959 for the opportunity to preach in a Communist-controlled country. But the idea seemed impossible. The Communists and the United States were hostile toward each other. Besides that, Communist countries promoted atheism, or the belief in no God, among their citizens. Many Communist countries were known for persecuting religious people. Graham himself had severely criticized communism as "inspired by Satan" since his Los Angeles crusade in 1949.[6] He doubted that Communists would ever consider letting him speak in their countries.

Yet, in 1967, he was granted a two-day visa to Yugoslavia, with permission to preach. The Yugoslavian government allowed no advance publicity or advertising for his visit. They were concerned that any large crowds Graham attracted could easily be provoked into an antigovernment demonstration. News about his trip had to be spread by word of mouth.

Upon his arrival in Zagreb, where he held his first service, Graham was greeted by Orthodox Church officials offering gifts of salt and bread—Yugoslav

Graham once described his rain-drenched service in Yugoslavia— a Communist country—as "the greatest meeting of my entire ministry."

symbols of welcome. His first service was in a soccer field outside the city. Rain poured, yet more than thirty-five hundred people came to hear him.

The Yugoslav audiences were small compared to the crowds he was used to elsewhere, but this was a Communist country. Graham described the service there as "the greatest meeting of my entire ministry."[7] In two days, he was able to preach to more than ten thousand people.

Graham avoided making any political statements while he was in Yugoslavia, saying, "I am not a repre-sentative of any government. I represent the Kingdom of God."[8]

In 1977, Graham visited Hungary. In that Communist country, religious repression was not as severe as in Yugoslavia, and church attendance was not prohibited. While there, Graham made an eight-day whirlwind tour of the country. His first service was at the Baptist Youth Camp at Tahi, near Budapest. He preached on a gently sloping hillside to fifteen thousand people. Hundreds had camped out all night to be there, and many had come from other Eastern European countries.[9]

Later that evening Graham spoke to a packed Sun Street Baptist Church in Budapest. Loudspeakers carried his message to those outside who could not fit inside the crowded church. At the end of the service, Graham was perplexed by a soft clicking sound he heard all over the church. Later he learned that it was the sound of dozens of tape recorders being turned off.[10] His listeners had recorded his message.

Stopping in a small Hungarian village, Graham and his wife were treated to authentic Hungarian goulash that had been cooked in a big pot over an open flame. Then the villagers encouraged him to try on a traditional shepherd's hat and ankle-length sheepskin cape. Before leaving, he was given a hand-made wineskin as a memento of his trip.[11]

Graham faced criticism in the United States for his willingness to speak in Communist countries. Many thought that he was being used by their governments. Favorable publicity showing pictures of Billy Graham in their countries could be used as propaganda to convince the rest of the world that Communist governments were more tolerant of religion and new ideas than they really were. But Graham was undaunted by such criticism.

He was also criticized because he was unwilling to condemn the Communist governments, as he had been so eager to do earlier in his career. He knew that if he criticized the Communist governments, he would never be granted permission to preach in their countries. So he decided to soften his criticism. "I've decided that if I am to have a world ministry, I'll have to leave political questions alone," he said.[12]

The year 1981 brought sadness to Billy Graham and his family when his mother died on August 14, after a period of declining health. He wrote, "Of all the people I have ever known, she had the greatest influence on me."[13]

In the 1980s, Graham emphasized world peace in his preaching. He also urged reconciliation between the United States, the Soviet Union, and China.[14]

In 1984, Graham received the invitation he wanted most—to preach in the Soviet Union. He had been hoping, praying, and working for this opportunity for twenty-five years. While there, Graham's strictly controlled tour allowed him to visit Leningrad (now St. Petersburg), Tallin in Estonia, Novosibirsk in Siberia, and Moscow.

Known for its repression and persecution of any religious expression, the Soviet government officially discouraged religion and promoted atheism. No advertising of Graham's visit was allowed, but loudspeakers were permitted for Graham's overflow crowds, even though there was a law against any kind of Christian evangelism outside church walls.[15] Still,

Ruth and Billy Graham enjoy a quiet moment in their comfortable, rustic home, Little Piney Cove. The bricks for the floor came from an abandoned schoolhouse, and the fireplace mantel was created from an old diving board that Ruth found at the town dump.

KGB agents (Soviet secret police) with cameras patrolled the services, intimidating listeners by their presence.

By 1982, Graham had hurdled every political and religious barrier to Christianity that he could find. From then on, his ministry only continued to build on its strong and broad foundation. With his gentle, accommodating spirit, and his sincere efforts for peace and understanding, Graham made himself and his message welcome in every culture throughout the world, regardless of the dominant religious or political views. He spent the next two decades continuing to do the work that he did best—preaching throughout the world. And he would preach to an ever-increasing number of eager listeners.

A Lasting Legacy

Billy Graham has preached the Gospel directly to more than 100 million people. He has preached on six continents, in eighty-four countries, and in all fifty states.[1] His picture has appeared on the covers of *Time, U.S. News and World Report, People, Newsweek*, and the *Saturday Evening Post* magazines. Sought after for interviews, he has been a frequent guest on a variety of talk shows, including *Merv Griffin, The Today Show, Good Morning America, Larry King Live*, and the *Johnny Carson Show*. He was also interviewed by the country's top journalists, including Dan Rather, Diane Sawyer, Peter Jennings, Sir David Frost, and Dick Cavett.

What is the secret of Graham's enduring appeal? Graham has said, "I'm no great intellectual, and there are thousands of men who are better preachers than I am. You can't explain me if you leave out the supernatural. I am but a tool of God."[2]

Others would say that Graham's appeal resulted from his certainty about his mission and his beliefs. He brought comfort and a sense of leadership to a realm where most are not certain but want to be. A *Time* magazine article noted that Graham's "sincerity, efficiency and unfaltering faith in his dependence on the power of God are far more important influences on the people who hear him than the things he says or the way he says them."[3] In addition, he has been one of the few evangelists to avoid scandal in their ministries. True to his Modesto Manifesto in 1949, Graham's fifty years of evangelism remained free from disgrace.[4]

Despite his success and overwhelming popularity, Graham has had his share of critics over the years. Liberal Christians have complained that he is too conservative.[5] Conservative Christians have complained that he is too open to liberal viewpoints.[6] Often he was accused of oversimplifying the Christian message.

Others have attacked Graham because he seemed to make becoming a Christian so easy. A *Time* magazine article reported that critics were saying his converts were only "Christians for a night."[7] Graham countered that concern with the effectiveness of his organization. Within twenty-four hours after a crusade, letters are sent to the church closest to each person who responds to Graham's invitation. That

More than 100 million people worldwide have attended Billy Graham's crusades.

way, a church is able to follow up with each new Christian.

Even so, in his later years Graham admitted that his sermons took on new emphasis over time. He said, "The cost of [being a] Christian . . . is coming more and more into my message now. This is where I think I failed in my earlier ministry. I didn't emphasize enough what it costs to follow Christ."[8]

Still another complaint about Graham's ministry has been the amount of money it costs to conduct a crusade. Graham responded by asking, "How do you evaluate the worth of a soul?"[9]

Graham has learned not to dwell too much on

criticism. He said, "When I was young, I sometimes wanted to answer all my critics. Now, I just leave them with the Lord. If I tried to answer every critic that's all I would have time to do."[10]

After fifty years, Graham's support organization continues to flourish. The Billy Graham Evangelistic Association has grown from a one-room office when it began in 1950 to a building that takes up nearly one square block. Today it has a staff of four hundred. One of the association's jobs is to arrange and organize Graham's crusades. The Spiritual Guidance Department answers the millions of letters it receives each year. Despite the organization's size and immense responsibilities, the staff begins each day with ten minutes of Bible reading and prayer.

Graham's ministry also continues with the books he has written. After his first book, *Calling Youth to Christ*, in 1947, he wrote twenty more volumes. Many of his books have sold more than one million copies and have remained on best-seller lists for weeks. His autobiography, *Just As I Am*, was published in 1997. Since then it has sold more than one and a half million copies. Altogether, more than 30 million copies of Graham's books have been sold worldwide. The royalty payments from his book sales go to Christian organizations and ministries.

Graham's first national telecast of his New York crusade was in 1957, and he continued to broadcast crusades and other special programs. He also set up regional phone centers staffed by trained volunteers who answered calls that came in during and after a televised crusade.

The Graham organization took advantage of satellite technology in 1985. Broadcasting from Sheffield, England, satellites were used to telecast Graham's crusade live to 230 auditoriums all over Great Britain. From that beginning, the use of satellite technology continued to expand. In 1995, Graham's Global Mission was telecast in 117 languages from the San Juan, Puerto Rico, crusade to three thousand locations in 185 countries and territories. "By using today's mass communications, we can preach to more people in one day than the Apostle Paul reached in a lifetime," said Graham.[11] His official Web site, www.billygraham.org, provides information about his life, ministry, and schedule.

Graham also donated money to establish the Billy Graham Center at Wheaton College. It is an international center of information, research, and training on Christian evangelism and missions. The center contains the Billy Graham Evangelistic Association archives, along with one of the world's largest libraries on evangelism and missions.

Graham's other lasting monument to his ministry is the Billy Graham Training Center at the Cove, near Asheville, North Carolina. Established in 1993, the Cove is a place for ordinary people who want to know more about the Bible. It consists of two inns, a chapel, and a training center where Bible study classes are held. In the summer, its grounds become a camp for children. This beautiful setting is where Graham intends to be buried.[12]

Graham also has an intense interest in training new evangelists to continue ministering throughout the world.[13] To create that opportunity, the Billy Graham Schools of Evangelism were set up. They are training conferences on evangelism for pastors and other Christian workers. Held in three- to four-day sessions, the conferences provide intense training in evangelism. They are held all over the world.

Graham's influence on individuals throughout his life has been immense. One particular area of impact has come from his relationships with U.S. presidents. Graham has had contact with every U.S. president since World War II. Not one to advise on political issues, Graham has said, "I feel my role is that of a spiritual counselor to men of all [political] parties."[14]

To honor his positive contributions, Graham has received hundreds of honors and awards from all over the world. A mountain was named for him in Nigeria, and a town was named for him in southern India. Charlotte, North Carolina, has named a highway for him. He has been honored by Jewish and Roman Catholic organizations. He also received the 1963 Gold Award of the George Washington Carver Memorial Institute to recognize his contributions to improving race relations.

Since 1955, in public-opinion polls conducted by the Gallup Organization, Graham has been listed among the ten most admired men. He was given a star on Hollywood's Walk of Fame. And he has received more than twenty-five honorary doctoral degrees from colleges and universities in the United States and in five foreign countries. In May 1996, he and Ruth received the Congressional Gold Medal, the

Graham has been a friend and spiritual adviser to many United States presidents, including Lyndon B. Johnson, right.

highest honor the U.S. Congress can award to a civilian.

In 1991, Billy Graham was diagnosed with Parkinson's disease. This progressively disabling disease causes increasing stiffness of the muscles and severe hand tremors. It also affects its victim's balance and coordination. With his advancing age and illness, Graham's walk became more halting. He found that he had difficulty writing, and there were days when his illness kept him in bed.

Over his fifty years of ministry, Graham's basic message did not change. Yet in his later years,

Graham's strict interpretation of the Bible softened. "I am far more tolerant of other kinds of Christians than I once was," he said.[15] In addition, he became less concerned about the number of people who respond to his invitation.[16]

In 1995, the board of directors of the Billy Graham Evangelistic Association unanimously elected Graham's older son, Franklin, as its first vice chairman. Although Franklin's teenage years were tempestuous and wild, he settled down as he grew into adulthood, becoming an ordained minister when he was twenty-nine years old. Franklin worked closely with the Billy Graham Evangelistic Association, directing a nonprofit missionary organization called

As he steps into his father's shoes, Franklin Graham, left, will continue to preach "the same message my father has faithfully proclaimed for fifty years."

Samaritan's Purse.[17] According to a 1996 *Time* magazine report, Franklin was next in line to assume leadership of the Billy Graham Evangelistic Association one day.[18]

By 1999, Billy Graham had reduced his crusade schedule to no more than two each year.[19] But he was not ready to retire completely. In the spring of 2000, Graham underwent surgery to relieve a buildup of fluid around his brain. He had to cancel a trip to Amsterdam in July, where he was scheduled to speak at a worldwide convention of evangelists. In November 2000, Graham announced that he was stepping down from his post as chief executive officer of the Billy Graham Evangelistic Association, and his son Franklin would take over.

Franklin Graham said he would continue to preach "the same message my father has faithfully proclaimed for fifty years. . . . we're not about to change it now or ever."[20]

Meanwhile, Billy Graham, age eighty-two, made it clear that he was not retiring. He still planned to speak at crusades in the United States, though he would no longer be able to travel abroad. "I don't know what the future holds," he has always said.[21] But the legendary "world's preacher," spiritual adviser and inspiration to millions, will preach as long as he has the strength.[22] He said his life is "dedicated to doing the work of an evangelist, as long as I live."[23]

Chronology

1918—William Franklin Graham II is born in Charlotte, North Carolina, on November 7.

1934—Graham's conversion at a religious revival meeting.

1936—Graduates from Sharon High School; enters Bob Jones College in Cleveland, Tennessee.

1937—Transfers to Florida Bible Institute, Temple Terrace, Florida; preaches his first sermon.

1940—Enters Wheaton College, Wheaton, Illinois.

1943—Accepts call as pastor of Western Springs Baptist Church, Western Springs, Illinois; graduates from Wheaton College; marries Ruth McCue Bell.

1944—First speaker for Chicagoland Youth for Christ; begins radio program, *Songs in the Night.*

1945—Resigns from Western Springs Baptist Church to work full-time for Youth for Christ.

1948—Becomes president of Northwestern Schools, Minneapolis, Minnesota; leaves Youth for Christ; World Congress of Evangelism sponsored by Youth for Christ, held in Switzerland.

1949—Holds a crusade in Los Angeles, California, which results in his first nationwide publicity.

1950—Establishes the Billy Graham Evangelistic Association; begins radio program, *The Hour of Decision;* forms Billy Graham Films (later renamed World Wide Pictures).

1952—Resigns from Northwestern Schools; begins "My Answer" newspaper column.

1953—Bans racial segregation at his crusades.

1954—First overseas crusade, in London, is a tremendous success.

1956—Founds *Christianity Today* magazine; purchases land and begins building a home, Little Piney Cove.

1957—Holds New York City crusade, attended by more than 2 million people; launches first televised crusade.

1974—Initiates an International Congress on World Evangelization held in Switzerland.

1977—Holds crusade in Hungry, a Communist country.

1983—Receives the Presidential Medal of Freedom, the nation's highest civilian honor; organization sponsors worldwide conference for evangelists, held in Amsterdam.

1985—Crusade broadcast over satellite network.

1993—Establishes the Billy Graham Training Center at the Cove, near Asheville, North Carolina; Graham is diagnosed with Parkinson's disease.

1996—Receives Congressional Gold Medal along with his wife, Ruth Graham.

1997—Publishes autobiography, *Just As I Am.*

2000—Names his older son, Franklin Graham, as the new chief executive officer of the Billy Graham Evangelistic Association but has no plans to stop preaching.

Chapter Notes

Chapter 1. "Puff Graham"

1. Marshall Frady, *Billy Graham: A Parable of American Righteousness* (Boston: Little, Brown and Company, 1979), p. 191.

2. William Martin, *A Prophet with Honor, The Billy Graham Story* (New York: William Morrow and Company, Inc., 1991), p. 115.

3. William Franklin Graham, *Revival in Our Time* (Wheaton, Il.: Van Kampen Press, 1950), pp. 122 and 151.

4. Billy Graham, *Just As I Am* (San Francisco: HarperSan Francisco and Zondervan, 1997), p. 147.

5. Frady, p. 202.

6. John Pollock, *Billy Graham: The Authorized Biography* (New York: McGraw-Hill Book Company, Inc. 1966), p. 55.

7. "Heaven, Hell & Judgment Day," *Time*, March 20, 1950, p. 72.

8. David Frost, *Billy Graham: Personal Thoughts of a Public Man* (Colorado Springs: Chariot Victor Publishing, 1997), p. 65.

9. Pollock, p. 56.

10. Graham, *Just As I Am*, p. 149.

11. Pollock, p. 61.

12. "Sickle for the Harvest," *Time*, November 14, 1949, p. 64.

13. "A New Evangelist Arises," *Life*, November 21, 1949, p. 97.

14. Graham, *Just As I Am*, p. 157.

15. Martin, p. 118.

Chapter 2. Farm Boy

1. William Martin, *A Prophet with Honor, The Billy Graham Story* (New York: William Morrow and Company, Inc., 1991), p. 57.

2. Morrow Coffey Graham, "My Son, Billy Graham," *Women's Home Companion*, October 1954, p. 90.

3. Ibid.

4. Marshall Frady, *Billy Graham: A Parable of American Righteousness* (Boston: Little, Brown and Company, 1979), p. 44.

5. Martin, p. 56.

6. Billy Graham, *Just As I Am* (San Francisco: HarperSan Francisco and Zondervan, 1997), pp. 12–13.

7. Ibid., p. 19.

8. Frady, p. 30.

9. Morrow Coffey Graham, p. 90.

10. William Franklin Graham, p. 18.

11. Frady, p. 48.

12. "Billy Graham: The Man at Home," *Saturday Evening Post*, Spring 1972, p. 47.

13. Ibid., p. 49.

14. John Pollock, *Billy Graham: The Authorized Biography* (New York: McGraw-Hill Book Company, Inc. 1966), pp. 3–4.

15. Morrow Coffey Graham, p. 90.

16. Martin, p. 61.

17. *Saturday Evening Post*, Spring 1972, p. 47.

18. Ibid.

19. Billy Graham, p. 25.

20. Ibid., p. 27.

Chapter 3. The Call

1. William Martin, *A Prophet with Honor, The Billy Graham Story* (New York: William Morrow and Company, Inc., 1991), p. 64.

2. Ibid.

3. Marshall Frady, *Billy Graham: A Parable of American Righteousness* (Boston: Little, Brown and Company, 1979), pp. 87–89.

4. Russ Busby, *Billy Graham, God's Ambassador* (New York: Time Life Books, 1999), p. 32.

5. Frady, p. 90.

6. David Frost, *Billy Graham: Personal Thoughts of a Public Man* (Colorado Springs: Chariot Victor Publishing, 1997), p. 150.

7. Billy Graham, *Just As I Am* (San Francisco: HarperSan Francisco and Zondervan, 1997), p. 35.

8. Ibid., p. 37.

9. Ibid., p. 38.

10. Martin, p. 67.

11. Frady, p. 93.

12. Martin, p. 66.

13. Graham, p. 39.

14. Frady, p. 99.

15. Ibid., p. 106.

16. Frost, p. 65.

17. Curtis Rist and Gail Cameron Wescott, "The Long Road Home," *People*, October 14, 1996, p. 133.

18. Martin, p. 75.

19. "Billy and His Beacon," *Newsweek*, May 1, 1950, p. 67.

20. Martin, p. 77.

21. John Pollock, *Billy Graham: The Authorized Biography* (New York: McGraw-Hill Book Company, Inc. 1966), p. 17.

22. Ibid.

Chapter 4. The Girl from China

1. Russ Busby, *Billy Graham, God's Ambassador* (New York: Time Life Books, 1999), p. 36.

2. Marshall Frady, *Billy Graham: A Parable of American Righteousness* (Boston: Little, Brown and Company, 1979), p. 134.

3. Ibid.

4. Ruth Bell Graham, *It's My Turn* (Minneapolis: World Wide Publishing, 1982), p. 50.

5. Frady, p. 136.

6. John Pollock, *Billy Graham: The Authorized Biography* (New York: McGraw-Hill Book Company, Inc., 1966), p. 25.

7. Patricia Daniels Cornwell, *A Time for Remembering: The Story of Ruth Bell Graham* (San Francisco: Harper & Row, Publishers, 1983), p. 59.

8. Morrow Coffey Graham, "My Son, Billy Graham," *Women's Home Companion*, October 1954, p. 91.

9. Cornwell, p. 61.

10. Ibid., p. 67.

11. William Martin, *A Prophet with Honor, The Billy Graham Story* (New York: William Morrow and Company, Inc., 1991), p. 84.

12. Ruth Bell Graham, p. 52.

13. Ibid., p. 59.

14. Busby, p. 38.

15. Cornwell, p. 80.

16. Busby, p. 39.

17. Interview with Nancy Jo Batman, October 6, 1999.

Chapter 5. The Sawdust Trail

1. George Marsden, ed., *Evangelicalism and Modern America* (Grand Rapids, Mich.: William B. Eerdmans Publishing Company, 1984), p. 15.

2. William Martin, *A Prophet with Honor, The Billy Graham Story* (New York: William Morrow and Company, Inc., 1991), p. 90.

3. Ibid.

4. Marshall Frady, *Billy Graham: A Parable of American Righteousness* (Boston: Little, Brown and Company, 1979), p. 160.

5. Russ Busby, *Billy Graham, God's Ambassador* (New York: Time Life Books, 1999), p. 40.

6. Ruth Bell Graham, *It's My Turn* (Minneapolis: World Wide Publishing, 1982), p. 78.

7. Billy Graham, *Just As I Am* (San Francisco: HarperSan Francisco and Zondervan, 1997), p. 100.

8. Busby, p. 41.

9. Martin, p. 96.

10. Ibid., p. 114.

11. Ibid., p. 102.

12. Frady, p. 160.

13. Marsden, p. 15.

14. Jeffrey K. Hadden and Anson Shupe, *Televangelism: Power and Politics on God's Frontier* (New York: Henry Holt and Company, 1988), p. 116.

15. Busby, p. 45.

16. Billy Graham, "Interview," *McLean's*, June 26, 1978, p. 6.

17. Busby, pp. 45–46.

Chapter 6. "The Bible Says . . . !"

1. William Martin, *A Prophet with Honor, The Billy Graham Story* (New York: William Morrow and Company, Inc., 1991), p. 113.

2. Curtis Mitchell, *Billy Graham: The Making of a Crusader* (Philadelphia: Chilton Books, 1966), p. 26.

3. Marshall Frady, *Billy Graham: A Parable of American Righteousness* (Boston: Little, Brown and Company, 1979), p. 192.

4. Billy Graham, *Just As I Am* (San Francisco: HarperSan Francisco and Zondervan, 1997), p. 143.

5. Stanley High, *Billy Graham: The Personal Story of the Man, His Message, and His Mission* (New York: McGraw-Hill Book Company, Inc., 1956), p. 147.

6. Frady, p. 204.

7. Patricia Daniels Cornwell, *A Time for Remembering: The Story of Ruth Bell Graham* (San Francisco: Harper & Row, Publishers, 1983), p. 87.

8. "Heaven, Hell, and Judgment Day," *Time*, March 20, 1950, p. 72.

9. Martin, p. 114.

10. Frady, pp. 192–193.

11. Tom Fesperman, *Charlotte News*, November 10, 1947.

12. Martin, p. 29.

13. Ibid., p. 124.

14. "Billy in Dixie," *Life*, March 27, 1950, p. 55.

15. *Time*, March 20, 1950, p. 73.

16. Ibid.

17. Martin, p. 136.

18. Ibid., p. 137.

Chapter 7. Building on Success

1. Richard H. Rovere, "Letter from Washington," *New Yorker*, February 23, 1952, p. 89.

2. William Martin, *A Prophet with Honor, The Billy Graham Story* (New York: William Morrow and Company, Inc., 1991), p. 143.

3. John Pollock, *Billy Graham: The Authorized Biography* (New York: McGraw-Hill Book Company, Inc., 1966), p. 101.

4. Billy Graham, *Just As I Am* (San Francisco: HarperSan Francisco and Zondervan, 1997), pp. 197–198.

5. Martin, p. 149.

6. Clarence W. Hall, "The Charisma of Billy Graham," *Reader's Digest*, July 1970, p. 92.

7. Billy Graham, "Billy Graham Makes Plea for an End to Intolerance," *Life*, October 1, 1956, p. 140.

8. Patricia Daniels Cornwell, *A Time for Remembering: The Story of Ruth Bell Graham* (San Francisco: Harper & Row, Publishers, 1983), p. 93.

9. Hall, p. 91.

10. "The Crusade for Britain," *Time*, March 8, 1954, p. 73.

11. Ibid.

12. Ibid., p. 72.

13. Russ Busby, *Billy Graham, God's Ambassador* (New York: Time Life Books, 1999), p. 77.

14. Cornwell, p. 98.

15. Ibid., p. 102.

16. Ibid., p. 105.

17. Ibid.

18. Busby, p. 79.

19. "34,586 Decisions," *Time*, May 31, 1954, p. 59.

20. Billy Graham, *Just As I Am*, pp. 235–237.

21. "Tour's End," *Newsweek*, May 31, 1954, p. 44.

22. Ibid.

23. "Prayer! Prayer! Prayer!" *Newsweek*, September 6, 1954, p. 45.

24. *Time*, October 25, 1954, cover.

Chapter 8. Glory in the Mountains

1. Patricia Daniels Cornwell, *A Time for Remembering: The Story of Ruth Bell Graham* (San Francisco: Harper & Row, Publishers, 1983), p. 112.

2. Ibid.

3. Russ Busby, *Billy Graham, God's Ambassador* (New York: Time Life Books, 1999), p. 70.

4. Ibid.

5. Ruth Bell Graham, *It's My Turn* (Minneapolis: World Wide Publishing, 1982), p. 62.

6. Ibid.

7. Ibid., p. 67.

8. Ibid., p. 84.

9. Ibid., p. 88.

10. Ibid.

11. Busby, p. 234.

12. Ruth Bell Graham, p. 106.

13. Curtis Rist and Gail Cameron Wescott, "The Long Road Home," *People*, October 14, 1996, p. 134.

14. Lelia C. Albrecht and Rick Lanning, "Billy Graham Has a Son, If Not a Successor, At Work in the Fields of the Lord," *People*, January 25, 1982, p. 28.

15. Billy Graham, *Just As I Am* (San Francisco: HarperSan Francisco and Zondervan, 1997), p. 267.

16. John Pollock, *Billy Graham: The Authorized Biography* (New York: McGraw-Hill Book Company, Inc., 1966), p. 163.

17. Billy Graham, p. 267.

18. "Billy Graham's India," *Newsweek*, August 13, 1956, p. 85.

19. "Billy in India," *Time*, February 13, 1956, p. 72.

20. Billy Graham, p. 271.

21. Pollock, p. 163.

22. William Martin, *A Prophet with Honor, The Billy Graham Story* (New York: William Morrow and Company, Inc., 1991), p. 221.

23. "A Mighty City Hears Billy's Mighty Call," *Life*, May 27, 1957, p. 20.

24. Billy Graham, "New York and I," *Look*, October 15, 1957, p. 37.

25. "God in the Garden," *Time*, May 27, 1957, p. 46.

26. "Special Religion Report," *Newsweek*, May 20, 1957, p. 66.

27. Busby, p. 89.

28. Marshall Frady, *Billy Graham: A Parable of American Righteousness* (Boston: Little, Brown and Company, 1979), p. 303.

29. "Held Over," *Time*, July 29, 1957, p. 48.

30. Frady, p. 315.

31. Billy Graham, "New York and I," *Look*, October 15, 1957, p. 38.

32. Frady, p. 316.

Chapter 9. Into All the World

1. "Billy Graham's World," *Newsweek*, March 28, 1960, p. 86.

2. "Moslems v. Billy," *Time*, February 15, 1960, p. 86.

3. "Billy's Bountiful African Harvest," *Life*, March 21, 1960, p. 28.

4. *Newsweek*, March 28, 1960, p. 86.

5. Ibid.

6. Kenneth L. Woodward, "Graham Goes East," *Newsweek*, August 29, 1977, p. 70.

7. "Graham Meets Communism," *Time*, July 21, 1967, p. 60.

8. Ibid., p. 61.

9. Billy Graham, "I Believe in God!" *Reader's Digest*, July 1978, p. 110.

10. Ibid., p. 111.

11. Ibid., p. 112.

12. Woodward, p. 70.

13. Billy Graham, *Just As I Am* (San Francisco: HarperSan Francisco and Zondervan, 1997), p. 711.

14. Harold Bloom, "The Preacher Billy Graham," *Time*, June 14, 1999, p. 197.

15. Richard N. Ostling, "Billy Graham's Mission Improbable," *Time*, September 24, 1984, p. 48.

Chapter 10. A Lasting Legacy

1. Russ Busby, *Billy Graham, God's Ambassador* (New York: Time Life Books, 1999), p. 99.

2. "The New Evangelist," *Time*, October 25, 1954, p. 55.

3. "God in the Garden," *Time*, May 27, 1957, p. 46.

4. Harold Bloom, "The Preacher Billy Graham", *Time*, June 14, 1999, p. 194.

5. "Billy in New York," *Time*, May 20, 1957, p. 104.

6. Richard N. Ostling, "And Then There Was Billy," *Time*, November 14, 1988, p. 86.

7. "Personality," *Time*, November 17, 1952, p. 47.

8. James Michael Beam, "I Can't Play God Anymore," *McCall's*, January 1978, p. 156.

9. "Billy Graham's Finale," *Newsweek*, July 22, 1957, p. 57.

10. Busby, p. 244.

11. Marshall Frady, *Billy Graham: A Parable of American Righteousness* (Boston: Little, Brown and Company, 1979), p. 285.

12. David Frost, *Billy Graham: Personal Thoughts of a Public Man* (Colorado Springs: Chariot Victor Publishing, 1997), p. 156.

13. Ibid.

14. "The Evangelist's Preacher," *Time*, November 4, 1968, p. 58.

15. Beam, p. 158.

16. Ibid., p. 156.

17. Lelia C. Albrecht and Rick Lanning, "Billy Graham Has a Son, If Not a Successor, at Work in the Fields of the Lord," *People*, January 25, 1982, p. 28.

18. David Van Biema, "In the Name of the Father," *Time*, May 13, 1996, p. 74.

19. Patricia Rice, "Minister Here Has Memories of Billy Graham's Crusades Going Back 50 Years," *St. Louis Post-Dispatch*, March 14, 1999, p. D7.

20. Jim Jones, "Billy Graham Places Ministry in Trusted Hands," *Fort Worth Star-Telegram*, November 29, 2000.

21. Clarence Hall, "The Charisma of Billy Graham," *Reader's Digest*, July, 1970, p. 92.

22. Curtis Rist and Gail Cameron Westcott, "The Long Road Home," *People*, October 14, 1996, p. 132.

23. William Martin, "Billy Graham," *Christian History*, 2000, vol. 19.

Further Reading

Busby, Russ. *Billy Graham: God's Ambassador*. New York: Time Life Books, 1999.

Daniels, Patricia. *A Time for Remembering: The Story of Ruth Bell Graham*. San Francisco: Harper & Row, Publishers, 1983.

Frady, Marshall. *Billy Graham: A Parable of American Righteousness*. Boston: Little, Brown and Company, 1979.

Frost, David. *Billy Graham: Personal Thoughts of a Public Man*. Colorado Springs: Chariot Victor Publishing, 1997.

Graham, Ruth Bell. *It's My Turn*. Minneapolis: World Wide Publishing, 1982.

Graham, Billy. *Just As I Am*. San Francisco: HarperSan Francisco and Zondervan, 1997.

———. *Revival In Our Time: The Story of the Billy Graham Evangelistic Campaigns*. Wheaton, Ill.: Van Kampen Press, 1950.

Martin, William. *A Prophet with Honor: The Billy Graham Story*. New York: William Morrow and Company, Inc., 1991.

Pollock, John. *Billy Graham: The Authorized Biography*. New York: McGraw-Hill, 1966.

———. *Billy Graham: Evangelist to the World*. San Francisco: Harper & Row, Publishers, 1979.

Walker, Jay. *Billy Graham: A Life in Word and Deed*. New York: Avon Books, 1998.

Wellman, Sam. *Billy Graham: The Great Evangelist.* Uhrichsville, Ohio: Barbour Publishing Co., 1996.

Westman, Paul. *Billy Graham: Reaching Out to the World.* Minneapolis: Dillon Press, Inc., 1981.

Internet Addresses

Billy Graham Evangelistic Association Homepage.

<http://www.billygraham.org>

"Heroes of History: Sam Wellman's Biography Site" has information and a reading list about Billy Graham.

<http://www.heroesofhistory.com/page52.html>

Time **magazine profile of Billy Graham.**

<http://www.time.com/time/time100/heroes/profile/graham01.html>

Index

Page numbers for photographs are in **boldface** type.